~ A Puget Sound Odyssey ~

By Daymond Speece

MAPS

PHOTOS

TABLE OF CONTENTS

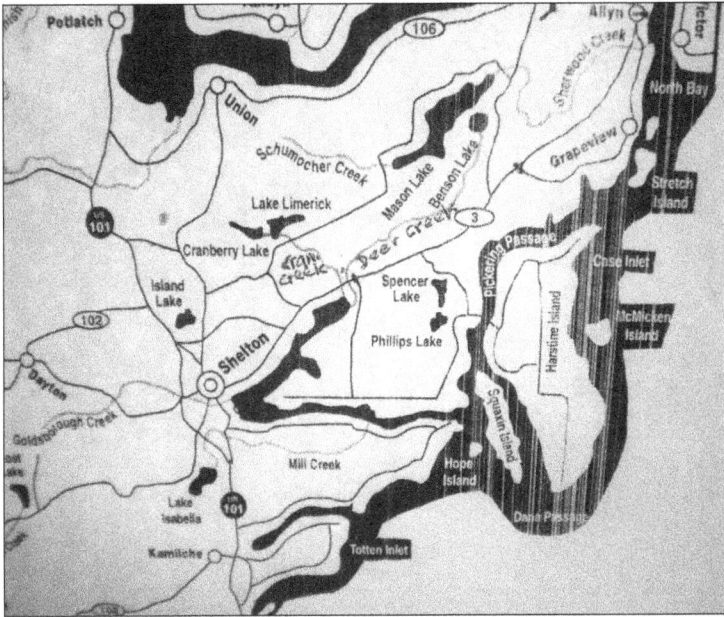

East Half of Mason County, Washington

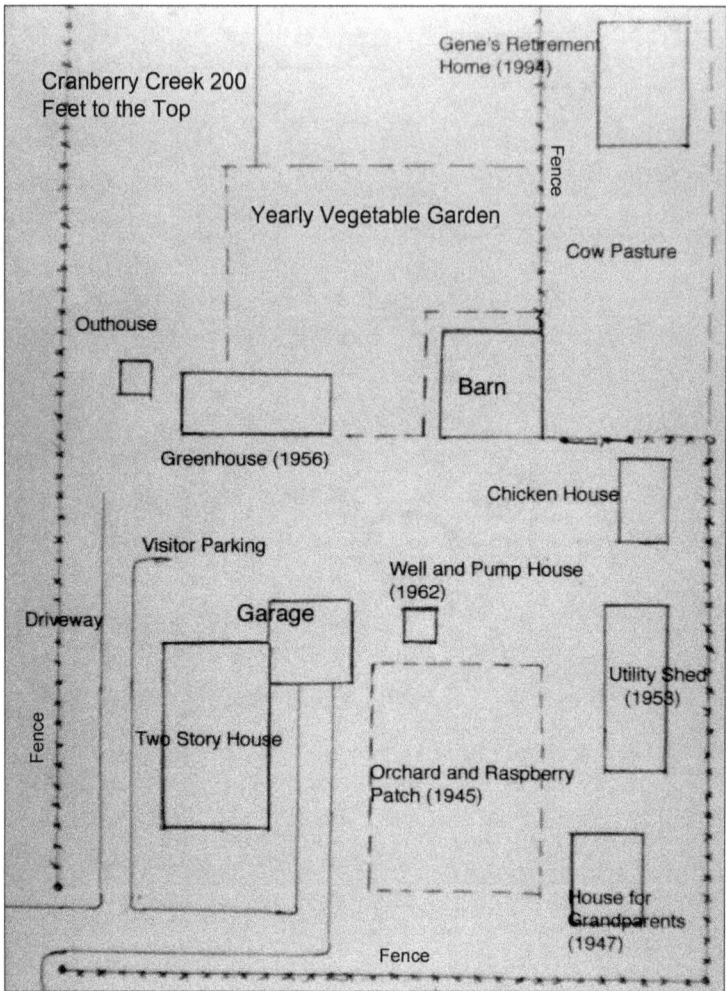

Speece Home at end of Cranberry Creek Road

Standing left to right: Lula, Leonard, Doris, Gene, Daymond
Seated left to right: Lucille, Neil, Marion (Lank)

Mom with our two baby bears.

Bear up a tree in our yard.

CAST OF CHARACTERS

Grandparents
Linus (1861 - 1955) and America Falls Speece (1867 - 1955)

Parents
Marion Roy Speece (9-19-07 to 10-7-60)
Lucille Adelaide (Cocherl) Speece (4-20-10 to 1-19-06)

Siblings
Leonard, born 8-25-30, married Ruth Mast
Gene, born 1-10-34; died 8-11-2006; married Hazel Lakim
Lula, 10 - 3 -34, married Jim Nichols
Doris 5-9-36; died 1-20-2013; married Keith Simpson
Neil 1938 - 1956

Uncle Louis Capalo 1909-1940
Aunt Edith (Speece) 1911-1985

Cousins
Jimmy Capalo 1932-1975
Daniel Capalo 1934

Neighbors and other players
Gossers: Lawrence, Eleanor, Larry, John

Slaters: Parents, Hewitt 1932, Ann 1933

Nasons:
Daughters Dorothy 1934, Mary 1935, Amy 1937 plus two older brothers

Cochrans: Mary, Fred, Eddie 1938, two younger daughters

~ *Preface* ~

This is my story of growing up in Mason County, Washington as I remember it. Because of my faulty memory, biased outlook, and tendency to exaggerate, this story may match the facts somewhat poorly in some areas.

My father, Marion Speece, was the youngest son of a ten-member Ohio family. In high school, he latched onto baseball as an activity in which he could outshine his two older brothers. He had two brothers who died at an early age. He married Lucille Cocherl shortly after his high school graduation and two years later moved to Mason County, Washington with his parents, newborn son (Leonard), wife, and two of his five sisters. He was delighted when his first three children were boys and imagined at least one of them becoming a famous athlete.

After he acquired a home of his own, he raised a large garden each year and hunted deer for meat. He tried to convince his sons that they should be self-sufficient and expert in these same areas. After a difficult several years of odd jobs during the Great Depression, he also wanted the boys to attend college and become well-paid professionals. Lucille concurred with this latter desire.

This autobiography documents the approximate antics and vignettes in the course of my survival through college and a few years beyond.

~ Heritage ~

In 1756 Conrad Spies was born in Mannheim, Germany.
In 1775, on shore leave from a German merchant ship, he
wooed and wed a German immigrant girl in New England.
They started a farm and had seven children. He changed
the spelling of his last name to Speece in an attempt to
anglicize it. I was told by a Speece I met at Lockheed that
the approximately 2000 Speeces in the world are direct
descendants of Conrad and Ann Catherine. About a third
of them live in Pennsylvania. Speecetown is a suburb of
Harrisburg in central Pennsylvania. He gave me a family tree
chart and asked where I fit in.

You can't always believe what you hear. In 1806 Jacob Spiece
was born in Hohensolm, Germany. He married Juliana in 1834
in Germany and they emigrated to the United States in 1839
with a son, Charles, and a daughter, Elizabeth. They settled
in Crawford County, Ohio, started a farm and had four more
children. To anglicize his name, Jacob changed it to Speece.
He was told by a neighbor that this was the American version
of Spiece.

In 1860, Charles Speece married Mary Dawson. In 1861 they
had a son, Linus Winfield Speece (my grandfather). Charles
joined the Union Army during the Civil War and was in
Sherman's Army during the March through Georgia. In
1884 Linus moved with his cousin to Vashon Island in Puget
Sound, Washington. In 1889 he had a job unloading ships in

Tacoma when he met and married 22-year-old America Falls (shortened to May) from Minnesota as she was visiting her sister in Tacoma. Linus filed for a homestead site on Mason Lake 12 miles northeast of Shelton, the county seat of Mason County, Washington. There in the next few years, as one of the first homesteaders on Mason Lake, Linus built a two-story log cabin, a barn, a woodshed, a root house, a wagon shed, a chicken house, and two small storage sheds. In Shelton he bought a horse, gun, stove, table, chairs, and bed and hauled them through the woods to his cabin.

In the 14 years they lived there, the couple cleared enough land to raise a garden, plant 175 fruit trees and have seven children. The first, a son, was born dead and another son died of spinal meningitis at the age of eight. The cabin was 14 x 28 feet with bedrooms on the second floor. Linus hunted deer and other wildlife to provide meat for his family. He got into politics and served as commissioner from the North District of Mason County from 1894 to 1898, then as assessor from 1899 to 1901. During this period he studied surveying and road building.

The first road from the county seat, Shelton, to Mason Lake (12 miles) and on to Allyn (plus 10 miles) was built under his direction. These secondary roads were built by the residents using their own time and teams.

By 1903, May Falls had become very unhappy with their isolated homestead, concerned about the time to get sick children to check-ups in Shelton, and tired of hearing about how lucky they were to be raising their family in such a lovely place. In the spring, Linus reluctantly sold the homestead, loaded up the old buggy with their most valued possessions and the children, and moved 10 miles northeast to Allyn. In 1905, after having another daughter, Mary Ella, they moved east. They acquired a farm near Marion, Ohio, to be near his relatives and "civilization." Here they had two more children, Marion and Edith. In 1931, they moved back to Allyn, Washington, where they retired.

The old growth forests around Puget Sound were truly majestic. They had the same awesome beauty as the old growth redwood forests in northern California. There was very little brush between the trees and room to drive a horse and buggy through. The Douglas Firs were up to 15 feet in diameter and 250 feet tall.

By 1886, Shelton was a logging town of several hundred people. It had 60 buildings including four saloons, two hotels, and two boarding houses for single loggers. The logging procedure included pairs of strong men working each end of a crosscut saw to fall and cut the forest giants into convenient lengths. Smaller trees were cut into six to ten foot lengths, peeled, greased, and laid out like railroad ties through the previously logged area. In marshy areas and across gulleys these were laid across longer logs, which maintained a level surface. They were called skid roads. Up to a half dozen teams of oxen or horses dragged the large logs along these skid roads and out on piers from which they were rolled into the waters of Puget

Sound. Some smaller logs were moved to the bay in "V" shaped flumes filled with diverted creek water. Sawmills were built on the Shelton waterfront with skid roads up from the bay and steam engines to drag the logs to the saws. The logging docks were built on logs pounded endwise into the bay bottom by a steam driven pile driver on a log raft which was towed into place by a tug boat.

Seattle initially had a logging industry and a skid road on the waterfront. As the city grew the sawmills were abandoned and the skid road area became a hangout for bums. Skid row entered the language as a synonym for a run-down sleazy part of any city.

By 1900 dirt roads connected the towns around Puget Sound. Family travel was by horse and buggy or water (sternwheelers). There was daily ferry service between Shelton and Olympia. Heavy goods moved primarily by water and rail. Shelton lumber moved by steamboat to Olympia, 15 miles away by water, which had the nearest cross-country rail terminal. Logs were roped together into large rafts and towed by tugboat to sawmills on Puget Sound. Steam engines, also known as donkey engines, were barged back to Shelton and used in the logging areas to drag logs from where they fell to the skid roads. The top and limbs were sawed off a large conveniently located tree (a spar tree) and a pulley was attached to the top about 30 to 50 feet off the ground. A heavy steel cable ran from a reel on the donkey engine through a pulley on top of the spar tree to a loop of cable (a choker) around one end of each newly cut section of log. The spar tree was held upright by cables to surrounding stumps. The donkey engine was bolted to a heavy slab of log and often blocked against a previously cut tree trunk (a stump) so that it could pull each large log out of the area where it fell and lift it onto a railroad car or a skid road instead of the choker cable dragging the donkey engine up to the spar tree and into the air. Railroad engines, cars, and rails were barged from Olympia to Shelton.

In 1902 several logging railroads were built from Puget Sound into the nearby forests to replace the skid roads. One line was built by the Satsop Railroad Company from the Shelton water front inland along the valley and extended as the logged off area progressed further inland. This was later acquired and extended by the newly formed Simpson Logging Company, which quickly became the major employer in Shelton and the third largest logging company on the Pacific Coast. In 1906 when San Francisco was rebuilding from its earthquake, Shelton claimed that more lumber was shipped from Shelton than from any other port in the world.

Shelton is at the end of a narrow eight-mile long westward running section of bay called Hammersley Inlet. At Shelton the inlet widens into Big Skookum Bay, which jogs to the northeast for three miles. Another two-mile extension is called Oakland Bay. The twice daily tides run as much as 15 feet from low to high tide. This tidal river washes up gravel beaches throughout Puget Sound except at the ends of the bays where mud from the winter floods of many streams accumulates.

Oakland Bay is a three-foot deep soft mud flat when the tide is out. Small creatures bake in the mud in the summer sun and create a memorable odor all around the bay.

The section of Puget Sound feeding Hammersley Inlet is called Pickering Passage and separates two large islands from the mainland. (Map p. 1) The nearest, Squaxin Island, is an Indian reservation. The larger three by ten mile Harstine Island is farther north. The little town of Allyn where I was born is 10 miles north of Hammersley Inlet near the end of the westernmost arm of Puget Sound (North Bay). By road along Oakland Bay, it is 18 miles from Shelton to Allyn and another 18 miles to Bremerton. The most frequent ferryboat service in Puget Sound is between Seattle and Bremerton. The Tacoma Narrows bridge provides a short route from Tacoma to Bremerton on to the eastern shore of Hood Canal.

At closest approach, north of Allyn, it is only four miles from the muddy end of Hood Canal to the muddy end of North Bay.

Until the late 1930s Shelton had signs on the main highways into town with large letters TNT. Below in smaller print they said "Travel Nigger Travel." Shelton was a Sundown town. No Negroes were allowed to be in town after sundown. During World War ll, these restrictions were cancelled.

~ *Our Family* ~

On March 17, 1929 my parents, Marion Speece and Lucille Cocherl, wed in Marion, Ohio. He was a 22-year-old farm boy, the youngest son of Linus and May Falls Speece. He had two older surviving brothers and five sisters. His mother named him after his place of birth to his eternal resentment. He grew to 6 feet 4 inches tall and went by Lank from teen age on. Mom, born in 1910, was the oldest daughter of an Irish greenhouse manager. She had four older brothers and a younger sister. One of her ancestors was in the Confederate army during the Civil War and an uncle was in the Ku Klux Klan.

For their honeymoon, Dad and Mom headed west to Los Angeles in a Model A Ford. After a spring of exploring and jackrabbit hunting in the high desert, they returned to Marion in 1930 where in August a son, Leonard, was born. In 1931 Dad's younger sister, Edith, married Louis Kapalo and they headed west with Dad, Mom, Leonard, Linus, May, and Dad's oldest and single sister, Mary Ella. Dad and his two sisters moved to remain near their parents.

Starting on August 31, 1931, it took 31 days, 220 gallons of gas per vehicle, (at 18 cents a gallon) and 35 quarts of oil (at 28 cents a quart) to drive three vehicles 3870 miles on dirt and gravel roads to Allyn, Washington. The passengers were divided between Louis's truck, Dad's Model A Ford, and Mary's sedan. On the first day a tire went flat on the sedan and the next morning a tire was flat on the truck. The next day the back axle on the truck broke. As the passengers were waiting for a repairman, who had been summoned from the next town by the sedan passengers, a Dodge sedan plowed into the back of the truck. Four days later the oil pump broke on the truck. That day they covered 50 miles. The next day the center front bearing failed on the truck after 23 miles.

On September 11, they drove 176 miles through a dust storm in South Dakota. Most nights they stayed with friends or relatives. In South Dakota they hunted pheasants after dark by chasing them across the fields with the truck and clubbing them. They killed 25 in two days and cooked them for breakfast for the next few days. There was a drought in western South Dakota and they drove through a thick cloud of grasshoppers. On the 21st day they entered the Wyoming Rockies and the weather turned cold. Mom and Leonard started riding in Mary's car, which was less drafty. In the final 10 days they had half a dozen flat tires on the truck.

They found that a bent rim was causing the flat tires. On September 30, seven miles south of Shelton and 25 miles from their final destination, the drive shaft on the truck broke.

In Allyn, the families settled near their parents' turn-of-the-century homestead. Edith and Louie had two sons, Jimmy in 1932 and Daniel in 1934.

Dad and Mom had three more sons: Eugene (Gene) in February 1932, and me, (named for a distant uncle, Raymond) in July 1933, and Neil in January 1938. By 1933, the Great Depression was at its height and both Dad and Louis had great difficulty finding enough part-time work to support their families. Both were heavy cigarette smokers. Dad quit but Louie bought a pipe, fastened a straight pin to the end of a stick, and retrieved enough cigarette butts from the streets to provide pipe refills and continue to support his habit. Both families raised gardens and obtained some help from Linus who had started a modest orchard. Dad killed and dressed deer as needed to provide a regular supply of venison. They both gaffed salmon from Sherwood Creek in the fall.

Dad and Mom had two daughters: Lula in October 1934 and Doris in May 1936. The family moved to a rental house on Hammersley Inlet near Shelton in 1937. The bayside home had wooden steps down a steep hill to the beach. Clams became a dietary staple and Dad acquired an almost seaworthy rowboat for fishing. Salt water salmon fishing is legal whereas using a large hook on a pole to gaff them in fresh water is not.

Native seals can be seen floating on driftwood in Puget Sound. There is a lot of driftwood because Shelton's main employer, the Simpson Logging Company, runs several mills and uses log rafts in the bay as storage areas. For many years the sawed off ends of the logs were dumped in the bay. Simpsons owned vast acres of second growth forest and, after the Depression, obtained government leases to log old growth Douglas Fir trees in Olympic National Park. Several logging trains and many trucks hauled their loads through Shelton each day and dumped them in the bay.

In the late '30s, Washington state paid a bounty of several
dollars for each pair of seal ears turned in. This program
was aimed at eliminating the seals because they dined on
fish including the fall salmon runs. They were regarded as a
general threat to the fish population. They liked to float in the
sun on the sawed off log ends (called lily pads). Many Puget
Sound residents, including Dad, shot the seals with rifles
as they drifted by. The state rarely paid the bounty because
wounded seals dived to the bottom and somehow stayed there
after they died and became crab and fish food.

Another threat to the salmon run was killer whales (orcas).
Packs of them sometimes followed the salmon run into Puget
Sound. Dad called them "black fish." One fall day as Gene and
I were anchored near shore fishing from the family rowboat,
some orcas swam close enough to terrify us. Gene hollered
at me to raise the anchor while he rowed frantically towards
shore. I couldn't pull it out of the gravel so he did it himself
after the whales had left. I was four years old and Gene
was five.

Dad built a sled for us boys and in the winter we took turns
sliding down the hill. One icy day after a sleet storm, Gene
and I were sliding rapidly towards the bluff to the beach when
Gene steered through the neighbor's barbed wire fence to
avoid flying off the bluff. The lower wire caught me by the neck

causing a rather nasty looking gash.

One afternoon, we four older children were out in the boat admiring the jellyfish floating by when Lula (two years old) fell overboard. Leonard and Gene managed to pull her back into the boat half drowned. At this point Mom decided that living by the bay was too hazardous to her children's health and too hard on her nerves. The family moved to another rental house several miles inland from Shelton.

~ *Moving Days* ~

From the Hammersley Inlet house on Puget Sound, we moved to a rental house in Dayton, eight miles inland west of Shelton. The family car was an old pickup truck with a chain across the back where the tailgate used to be. We three older boys sat in the back with our feet dangling and held onto the chain. Mom controlled the girls in the front seat and Dad drove.

In 1938 there was massive unemployment and limited welfare (mostly flour, sugar, salt, wheat, and rice distribution through the public schools). Dad worked at whatever odd jobs he could find – mostly mowing hay, plowing gardens, or clearing brush using various borrowed horses. The pay was usually in garden produce, milk, or eggs. Mom maintained a small garden and a few chickens. Dad had a 22-caliber rifle and a 30-30 rifle and killed deer as needed throughout the year and cut up the venison for meat. He used the 22 for out-of-season (illegal) hunting because it made very little noise. There was neither electricity nor cooling other than creek water and cold weather, so steaks needed to be cooked and eaten rather rapidly. A neighbor had goats and our family became accustomed to goat milk.

As the oldest son, Leonard received a disproportionate amount of Dad's attention and developed a feeling of superiority and control over the younger children. For lack of neighboring children, Leonard played mostly with Gene and both teased me when I tried to join in their activities. The girls played with each other.

In the 1936-37 school year, Leonard attended grade school in Shelton and hated every minute of it. He particularly hated the older boys who showed him no respect and beat him up frequently. At the end of the year, the school recommended that he repeat the first grade since he seemed to have learned very little. Dad and Mom agreed provided that Gene be allowed to start the first grade at age five and a half in the fall so Leonard would have someone familiar to commiserate and play with. Mom resolved to tutor both of them as necessary to guarantee satisfactory progress. From first grade on, they became inseparable buddies.

On January 3, 1938, another son, Neil, was born. Initially he was ignored by the boys and babied by the girls. When he reached the crawling stage all the older siblings tried to avoid him.

Mom was in charge of cooking, house cleaning, the garden, washing the clothes and kids, and sewing up holes in clothes to extend their wearability. For clothes washing, she had a galvanized tub and a rub-a-dub washboard. The clothes were dried on an outside clothesline in sunny weather and inside during the rainy season.

The wash tub was filled with heated water each Saturday night and the kids were bathed in sequence followed by the adults. The water was heated in a boiler pan on the kitchen stove. The boiler was also used for canning garden vegetables in the fall and fruit whenever enough could be obtained, usually from Grandpa's orchard or in partial payment for Dad's part-time jobs. Family moves were usually in the winter after the garden was finished.

The annual rainfall around Shelton is about 70 inches and water was usually available via a cast iron hand pump from a 10 to 15 foot deep hand-dug well near each house. The privy (outhouse) was usually a one or two holer over a hand-dug pit beyond smelling distance from the house. This provided an incentive not to eat or drink anything after dinner in the evenings, especially in the winter.

The Dayton house was too small to comfortably fit our growing family, and Mom was prodding Dad to borrow enough to start buying a larger permanent home. At the end of December 1937, Dad obtained a $600 loan from a Shelton lawyer who he had cleared land for, and who had befriended the family. He bought a two story frame house on five acres near the end of Oakland Bay with agreement that the loan could be repaid as his meager earnings permitted. The new home had been built by the Skinner family along with a barn, a garage, a chicken house, and two acres of cleared land including a quarter acre which had been plowed and used as a vegetable garden.

The entry to the new house was through the kitchen. The upstairs became a bedroom for us three older boys and the primary storage area. There were two additional bedrooms downstairs, our parents slept in one and our sisters and Neil in the other. The two larger downstairs rooms became the dining room and family room. There was a centrally located brick chimney with two holes for stovepipes. The Skinners left a 100-gallon oil drum mounted on its side with welded iron legs, a stovepipe to the chimney, and a sliding plate opening for wood as a central heating unit. Another stovepipe came from a cast iron wood burning stove in the kitchen. Since it had a flat top it was used for cooking and heating water.

Our living room table was a crude picnic type table about seven feet long with built-in benches on each side. It was made of low-grade second-hand lumber and placed under the side window in the living room to provide natural lighting for daytime meals. Dad sat at one end with Leonard and Gene to either side so that he could backhand them when necessary. Mom sat at the other end with the girls and fed Neil who was seated in a homemade high chair. I was on the side with my back to the wall so that I couldn't get away. The older kids served themselves. We all played with our food. I liked to center mine on my plate. If we had peas, beans, or other multi-items as opposed to glop food (like mashed potatoes or meat), I would place the individual peas or whatever in a neat circle around the rest of the food. This annoyed Dad but not enough to disrupt the meal over it. Once when we had raw carrots, Dad took out his pocketknife and sliced some pieces off so Leonard took out his pocketknife and carved a small boat. As he put it in his mouth, he said "Down my throat and through my tubes, this little boat will sail for many a day." Dad almost backhanded him but instead said, "Shut up and eat your dinner."

As Dad made additional trips to move all of the family possessions, we boys began exploring. The walls were only partially finished and on one 2 by 4 someone had scrawled, "Dear Ferd, I have such a hard time." We never did find out who Ferd was.

Across a decrepit barbed wire fence from the house were the ashes of a burned Christmas tree with some undamaged colored glass ornaments. We carefully gathered these and presented them to Mom. Our Christmas trees had always been decorated with cookies, popcorn strings, and colored paper chains.

At the far end of the cleared field was an abrupt drop-off of about 10 feet to Cranberry Creek. The Skinners had used this drop-off as a garbage dump, which we boys sifted through at our leisure. It was mostly empty food cans and broken dishes, but I found a silver plated teaspoon, which I presented to Mom and proclaimed it "the prettiest spoon I ever saw".

Cranberry Creek ran from Cranberry Lake about four miles up in the woods into Oakland Bay. It was about half the size of California's Sacramento River at Dunsmuir above Shasta Dam. About half a mile from the new Speece home in the opposite direction was the slightly larger Deer Creek. Both streams were partially choked with old fallen trees, which were rotting away. Both had heavy fall salmon runs. These streams during winter floods were the primary source of the deep mud throughout Oakland Bay. Both were lined with forests of alder, maple, cedar, and hemlock. Both were paralleled by decaying skid roads left over from the old growth logging near the turn of the century. Deer Creek still had a stand of old growth Douglas Fir visible from our house. This was logged during World War II.

Our new home was one-fourth mile from the main paved Shelton Road to Bremerton Highway, which passed through Allyn 18 miles from Shelton. Our nearest neighbors were the Castles halfway to the highway. They had built a dam across Cranberry Creek and a wooden flume to carry water to a turbine driven electric generator. Theirs was the only local house with electric lights until electric lines were strung out along the bay from Shelton in the late '30s. The Castles also had an abandoned sawmill, which greatly impressed us.

Our other neighbors within half a mile were the Nasons across Cranberry Creek, the Pauls near the Castles, and the Casteels near Deer Creek.

We used a kerosene lamp for nighttime lighting until about 1942 when Dad got permission to extend electric lines to our house. In the late '30s one of the Oakland Bay residents bought a used single seated seaplane. It was essentially a Piper cub with pontoons. He took off and landed on the bay. He visited us one afternoon and talked about flying. This also impressed us.

~ Chickens, Pets, Fish and Other Animals ~

After we moved into the Skinner house, Dad acquired a cow and rebuilt the Skinner's barbed wire fence around three sides of the property. The woods along Cranberry Creek were left unfenced so the cow could find water. She would get lost about milking time every evening and Dad would send us boys to bring her back to the barn. He had her bred in the fall and the next year we had two cows and twice as much fun. When the new calf was born, Doris adopted it as a pet. The barn initially had no mangers or milking areas. Dad built a fir pole add-on with two mangers. Hay was put in these at milking times to distract the cows from the milking operation. About a quarter mile up Cranberry Creek, he found a fallen cedar tree. He took a crosscut saw and had Leonard help him saw it into two-foot lengths. He split these with a sledgehammer and wedge to make shingles that he used to roof his add-on. This was the most common roofing technique in rural western Washington at the time.

When we moved in to our new home, a neighbor gave Mom a few chickens and we always had eggs for breakfast and fryers as an alternative meat to venison and salmon. Dad would have us boys clean the chicken house and spread the leavings on the garden plot. He borrowed a horse to plow it each spring and helped Mom plant rows of climbing beans and peas along chicken wire fences and rows of carrots, corn, onions, lettuce, potatoes, beets, tomatoes, strawberries, kale, and miscellaneous other vegetables. The kale was used for cole slaw. The garden did not get watered and did poorly in dry summers.

A 20-foot square area behind the chicken house was fenced with a six-foot high wire mesh. There was an opening to this yard at the back of the chicken house. The chickens kept their yard picked clean of every blade of grass and the gravel provided grist for their craws. The craw is a pouch of gravel that the food passes through on the way to the stomach. Since chickens don't have teeth, the craw serves a grinding molar type function. The giant leaf- eating dinosaurs also had craws, but their grit consisted of softball size river rocks (gastroliths). These have been found in place with dinosaur skeletons. Rocks formed of the digested food waste, which passed through the other end and petrified, are called coprolites.

Once a neighbor donated some bantam chickens to Mom. These are quail sized chickens. Unfortunately, they all flew over the chicken wire fence and were last seen roosting in trees by Cranberry Creek. Another neighbor donated a tom turkey that lived in the yard and liked to chase the girls and me into the house until we got our revenge at Thanksgiving time (with Dad's help).

Another time, Dad was given a young pig in partial payment for some work. He built a small wooden pen by the chicken pen for the pig and lined the bottom edges with partially buried six-inch diameter logs. The pig rooted his way under one of these and ran into the woods. It came back at feeding time and Dad tossed it back into its pen and plugged the holes with rocks. It dug another hole and escaped again. This time Gene caught it and Dad killed and butchered it. We never had another pig, bantam chicken, or turkey.

Some of the chicken eggs were hatched, to replenish the chicken population. Dad built a chicken wire pen covered at one end to keep out the rain. It was about 4x6 feet long and 2.5 feet high with a flap that opened in the top. The baby chickens were fed discarded supermarket greens which Dad hauled home from Safeway. We sometimes caught crickets and tossed them in to watch the chicks scramble for them. During thunder storms and some cricket pursuits most of the chicks would run and pile up in an outside corner of the pen and suffocate the bottom third of the group. Chickens have always seemed to me to be the epitome of stupidity.

One spring the cow had a bull calf. After it was weaned that summer (not allowed to feed from its mom's teats anymore), Dad castrated it. He threw the parts into the garden. I found the scrotum and carried it into the house. I showed it to Mom and said, "Look, some little animal jumped clear out of its skin!" Mom discarded the little fur piece with no comment.

That fall, I was assigned the chore of staking the calf in the garden and moving it each day to a new grass supply. It was tied by a 10-foot long rope to a sharpened wooden stake, which was pounded securely into the ground with a sledgehammer. By winter, the calf was dragging me between stake locations instead of the other way around. One night a rainstorm and hard freeze left a 10-foot diameter ice patch in the garden. As I started to move the calf, it galloped at top speed out onto the ice patch. As I pulled on the rope, it slid and fell down. Each time it got up, I had circled to the far side of the ice patch and jerked on the rope to knock it down again. When it was thoroughly exhausted, I dragged it to the edge of the ice patch and staked it there.

For butchering cows, Dad fastened a sturdy crossbar about 10 feet up between two fir trees at the edge of the field. He fastened pulleys to his crossbar about six feet apart. He led the cow out under this and killed her with a 30-30 shot to the neck. Then he fastened a rope through each pulley to each hind leg. He fastened the other ends to his front car bumper and hauled the carcass into the air by backing up the car. Then he slit her throat, gutted her, skinned her, and cut her into steaks. He used a butcher's saw to cut through bones. The guts, hide, and head were rolled into a pre-dug hole and buried. The entire process had to be finished in one day or the coyotes would drag the hide and guts off.

The Western Washington deer only weigh about 100 pounds. The preferred way to kill one of them was with a neck shot. Then the throat was cut and the whole thing gutted and beheaded on the spot. Its hind legs were then tied to its front legs and it was hoisted onto the hunter's back with the legs around his neck like a backpack. This was called cross toggling. The deer was then carried to the hunter's vehicle, hauled home, strung up by its hind legs, skinned, cut into steaks, and stored. If our venison supply ran low and it was not hunting season, Dad would kill a deer in the local woods, cart it directly home, hang it in the garage, skin it, and cut it into steaks. The skin and other evidence were buried the next day. The coyotes dragged off the head and guts overnight.

A chicken was killed by holding it by its legs with its head on a block of wood and beheading it with a hatchet, hanging it up by its hind legs until it quit bleeding, then dunking it in scalding water, pulling all the feathers out, singeing off the hair, cutting it up, and storing it in the refrigerator. Dad did the catching and beheading and Mom did the rest. Leonard was eventually assigned the job of beheading chickens. On his first effort, he let go of the legs after the head was severed, and the chicken flopped around the yard until he caught it again. Several times he inflicted gory wounds without severing the head. But he eventually became fairly proficient at it.

~ *The Grade School Years* ~

In January 1938, Leonard and Gene transferred from the Shelton grade school six miles away in Shelton to the Oakland Bay grade school a mile towards town from our house. It was a one-room schoolhouse with a crippled (arthritic) teacher, Mrs. Hoffman, who taught about 15 kids in grades one through six. Some of the boys were hard to control although she tried.

The school facilities included an outdoor privy. One of the older boys found a low spot behind it from which he could observe the bottoms of the users. He cut himself a long willow switch one recess period, and used the twigs on the end to tickle the bottoms of the girls after they were seated. He was having a great time until he used it on the teacher. She came clumping out the door using her metal walker, which she used for walking. She hurried around to the back while pulling up her panties and grabbed him by the leg. After thumping him in the head for a while, she sent him home with instructions not to come back until he had his parents with him. They may not have cared much because we don't recall his ever coming back. After the end of the school year in June, she didn't come back either. The teacher for the next year when Leonard and Gene were in second grade was Mrs. Layton. I started in the first grade the following year (1939).

Once a hunter donated a butchered bear to the school. It was the end of the month and the government supplies were being doled out. So each kid who wanted one also got a bear steak to take home. It was tough meat with a strong taste. Two things I have never liked were bear meat and goat milk.

On one food distribution day, two of the older boys had a fight at recess. The older of the two vowed to beat the other boy's brains out after school. As Leonard and Gene were walking home along the highway, they saw the remains of a bag of rice with which one of the boys had bopped the other over the head. They decided that they must have been looking at the younger boy's brains.

In Western Washington, as elsewhere, the legal deer-hunting season is in the fall. But Dad hunted whenever the family meat supply got low. In the spring of 1938, Dad was arrested while putting a dead deer in the bed of his pickup and spent a month in the Mason County Jail in Shelton. The sheriff provided him with a card deck and taught him about a dozen games of Solitaire. After his release, he passed most of these on to his family.

Lawrence Gosser was the most active member of the Oakland Bay School Board and was a member of the Mason County Civil Service Commission. He established an oyster business on Puget Sound and lived near his oyster-opening house on the end of Oakland Bay. He befriended Mom when Dad was in jail and became a family friend. He had two married brothers who also lived along Oakland Bay. His brother, Ronald, became part of Dad's annual fall deer hunting party. His other brother Donald's oldest son Donald (Donny) started grade school with me in the Fall of 1939 when Leonard and Gene started the third grade. Most of the grade schoolers walked along the highway to and from the school.

Miss Willis was the Oakland Bay grade school teacher for the next dozen years. She believed in cracking knuckles with the edge of a ruler to control boisterousness and maintain attentiveness. In her first year, she bought a new Ford sedan for $600, which greatly impressed us. Most of our families were subsisting on part time work.

I was used to being teased and bullied by my older brothers and received more of this from the other boys in grade school. The schoolyard had several tall fir trees and I would climb one of these and look at the bay and Shelton during most recesses. Leonard and Gene volunteered to Mom to help me learn my ABCs, which gave them a chance to copy Miss Willis's knuckle rapping technique. I eventually found that I could get written teachers' commendations for good school reports. After I learned to read, I spent many recesses in the school library. I spent some winter evenings reading by the light of a kerosene lamp. Homework was minimal and was usually completed at school as Miss Willis was teaching one of her other five grades.

A romance blossomed between a first grade girl and me. We would sit in some hidden spot at recess and vow eternal love to each other. It was interrupted by summer vacation and she didn't come back in the fall.

The grade school central heating system was a pot bellied wood burning stove in the center of the classroom. Once someone tossed several 30-30 rifle shells into the fire. The resultant banging and clanging held the class's attention for a while.

Occasionally Miss Willis would smell a fart. She would ask the class "who passed gas?" Sometimes an adjacent student would finger the guilty party who would then be ordered to stand, apologize to the class, and run around the school building before sitting down again.

Most of the time no one would speak up. Then Miss Willis would have the whole class file out, run around the school building, and sit down again before continuing their activities.

During recess, the kids were supposed to stay on the school grounds but a few of the boys sometimes crossed the highway and had contests to see who could skip a rock the most times in the bay, or if the tide was out, who could throw a big rock the farthest out into the mud and make the biggest splat.

One sunny day as I was walking home from school, I decided to see how hard it would be to wade through the bay mud. I cut across a narrow part of the mud flat sinking in up to my crotch and nearly losing a shoe as I pulled each leg up for the next step. When I got home, caked with smelly mud up to my waist, my mother stripped and bathed me and administered half a dozen reasons to my rear end to avoid repeating this performance.

One day I noticed a sack of sugar in the kitchen. Trying to impress my Mom with my school learning, I announced that I knew how to spell "cigar." When Mom asked, I said "s-u-g-a-r".

In the 1940-41 school year, Lula started in the first grade, I was in the second grade, and Leonard and Gene were in the fourth grade. One icy day on our walk to school, we crossed the highway on a curve to stay on the sunny side of the street. Lula was last and was hit by a car that slid on the ice when it saw us and braked on the curve. The driver took her home and apologized profusely. We thought she was pretty lucky because she got out of school for a few days until the bump on her head went down.

The Paul family lived in a small one-bedroom house half way to the highway from us. They had a daughter near my age. One day as she was walking home from school with us, she asked if we knew what caused women to have babies. When we shook our heads "no", she pulled down her panties, pulled up her dress, pointed to her vagina, and said, "It happens after a man pees right here." Thus we got our first bit of sex education. Another time she asked us if we knew what made the ocean roar. She informed us that we would roar, too, if we had that many crabs on our bottoms. Unaware of any double meaning (crabs is slang for a venereal disease), we spread this story to everyone we knew.

When Donny Gosser and I were the entire fifth grade, Miss Willis decided that a two- pupil grade with an over-achiever, and an under-achiever didn't make sense. So she promoted me to the sixth grade and demoted Donny to the fourth grade. This ended any effort by Donny to learn school stuff. From heckling by older boys including my brothers, I developed an inferiority complex about my physical abilities that lasted into college. Through high school, I was a year or two younger and smaller than my classmates and always chosen last for any physical education team. But I was always near the top of the class scholastically.

The Oakland Bay Grade School had several second growth fir trees on the grounds. These were about two feet thick at the base and 70 feet high. During recesses, I usually climbed one of these and admired the view that included the pulp and paper mill smoke stack in Shelton five miles away. One day as I started to climb down, a limb broke off and I tumbled down through the branches to the ground. The following year, as a result, the trees were removed.

~ Summer and Weekend Activities ~

We three boys spent most of our summers exploring the woods along Cranberry Creek and Deer Creek and admiring the decaying skid roads. There was a large brushy marsh area along Deer Creek known as Deer Creek Swamp, where the skid road had been mounted about three feet above the mud on pilings driven into the gravel below. We practiced walking along the parts of the skid road that were still standing. The area had thick stands of alder and vine maple trees, stinging nettles, and devils club. The latter are in brushy clumps and have a dense layer of barbed thorns on each branch. If you grabbed a devils club to keep from falling down, the thorns would break off in your palm and sometimes work their way through to emerge from the back of your hand.

The woods along both creeks had numerous deer and a few black bears. A neighbor, Ira Casteel, became friendly with Dad and they hunted deer together in the adjacent woods throughout the year. His son, James, was Leonard's age and became a good friend to Leonard and Gene. Buddy Knutsen was another good friend from grade school.

The Knutsens lived two miles up Cranberry Creek. Buddy had an older blond sister and a younger blond sister. Their mother started a Sunday school for local children. In good weather, we boys would trudge through the woods both ways to attend Sunday school. I thought both of Buddy's sisters were beautiful.

The second growth forests in western Washington have thick growths of huckleberry brush averaging nearly five feet tall. The huckleberry is a smaller relative of the blueberry and makes tasty pies and cobblers. Each berry is about one-fifth inch in diameter and picking them individually would be very tedious. Dad's approach was to place the family washtub under one bush after another, then beat each bush with a club. After about an hour, he would have several inches of tub bottom covered with ripe and green huckleberries, twigs, leaves, spiders, etc. He would then carry the tub home and fill it with cold water. Mom and us boys would scoop off and discard anything that floated to the top. Most of the ripe berries would sink. A little additional sorting would produce several quarts of relatively clean huckleberries.

Wild blackberries were another delicacy and the vines spread rapidly in newly logged areas. The whole family spent numerous afternoons partially filling empty coffee cans with wild blackberries. The younger generation consumed two berries for each one which ended up in their coffee cans and ate most of the latter on the way home. Dad didn't object very vocally because our cans contained more green berries and twigs than ripe berries. He liked to tell us that when a blackberry is red, it's green.

Mom was a talented berry picker. A local winery hired people to pick logan berries, grapes, raspberries, etc., when the berries were ripe. The pickers were paid by the quantity picked. One summer Mom got rides to the berry patches with a neighbor while Dad found part time work elsewhere. Dad took Leonard, Gene, and me with him while Mom had the younger three children with her on days when they both worked. On days when Dad didn't have another job, he would drive the family to the berry patch and also pick berries.

The woods around the berry field had patches of poison oak. One afternoon I wandered into the woods to relieve myself and wiped on poison oak leaves. I did not do that again.

Even in hard times we seemed to always have iodine and cough syrup. Any wounds or rashes, including poison oak, were treated with iodine. One day Leonard and Gene were playing with a discarded bicycle inner tube from the Skinner dump. They lit it afire and Leonard was swinging it around in the air. Gene was standing too close and the burning rubber wrapped around his neck. This, too, was treated with iodine. One day, I jumped off the barn roof and landed on a rusty nail protruding upward from a discarded board and drove it through my foot. This was also treated with iodine. Another time Neil was sucking on an empty 22- rifle cartridge and swallowed it. As he was apparently choking on something, Dad and Mom rushed him to the hospital in Shelton where it was identified from an x-ray and allowed to follow nature's movement out. This was one of the few cases which was not treated with iodine or cough syrup.

The older two teased the rest of us kids a lot. A favorite pastime was to chase the girls while swinging a garter snake by the tail. These are harmless foot-long snakes, which live in the grass and eat insects. Western Washington has somewhat larger water snakes which eat small fish and frogs. We occasionally hooked one of these when we were trout fishing. The area has red anthills on the edges of the woods. These are typically about a foot high and two feet wide at the base and swarming with ants. A lot of garter snakes were tossed on anthills over and over until the ants killed them and picked the skeletons clean.

The older boys noticed the resemblance between Dad's umbrella and a parachute. They got on the barn roof with the umbrella and me. I was about eight years old. They decided that, being the lightest, I should test it. They positioned me over the cow manure pile to avoid damage from a hard landing and pushed me off, umbrella in both hands. The experiment did not seem to be a success since I shot into the manure pile in free fall and buried myself up to the waist. They talked me into going to the creek and rinsing myself before I entered the house. They replaced the umbrella and denied any knowledge of my whereabouts. Mom's reaction when I entered the house was to strip me, scrub my clothes, have me take a bath, put on clean clothes, and spank all three of us

That fall, Dad fastened gaff hooks to six-foot long poles and sent the older boys off to Cranberry Creek to gaff salmon. This became a fall weekend activity for us boys until we were in high school. One day as we were walking along the highway from Cranberry Creek to Deer Creek with our gaff hooks, we were stopped by a game warden who confiscated our gaff hooks and gave us a lecture on our criminal activity. We started to cry so he drove us two miles to the Bayshore Store and bought each of us an ice cream cone. He drove us home and gave a lecture to Mom. When Dad got home, he fashioned new gaff hooks for us and warned us to stay off the highway. We were gaffing salmon again the next weekend.

During another gaffing session, I leaned my pole against a fallen log. As I started to climb over it, I bumped the pole and it slid off the log and gaffed me through the wrist. One of the older Nason boys heard the ruckus and used his pocketknife to remove it, leaving a lifelong scar on my wrist.

One day as Leonard and Gene were trying to gaff some salmon between logs in a deep hole, a neighbor's boy, Eddie Cochran, was trying to stab those escaping upstream with a pitch fork. As they moved to another hole, he commented that his foot was getting cold. He had stabbed a pitchfork tine through his boot and foot.

The salmon swim up the west coast creeks and rivers when they are four years old to spawn and die. The females wallow in the gravel as they lay their eggs, then the males wallow among the eggs as they disperse their sperm. This way about a tenth of the fertilized eggs get buried in the gravel to produce a new generation of salmon while the rest are smashed by the parents or drift downstream. The salmon run is followed by steel head ocean trout that eat the loose eggs and by ducks that eat the rotting salmon after they die.

In the spring, the young salmon swim to the bay and ocean to return to the same stream in four years. The salmon seem to be acutely sensitive to trace elements, which uniquely fingerprint their stream. They will not swim up any other stream.

Another illegal and uncommon way to catch salmon was to take dynamite into the bay in an open boat (rowboat). The procedure was to light a stick of dynamite and throw it as far as you could. When it explodes, you row over and net the stunned salmon into the boat. Sometimes the dynamite exploded before it was thrown and the fisherman fed the fish.

In the summer of 1941, Dad had a week-long job using a horse and cable to pull brush and extend a field near where the Northern Pacific railroad spur, used by the Simpson Logging Company to ship lumber, passed over Mill Creek on its way to Olympia. He took us boys along with him for several successive days to give Mom a rest. When we got tired of watching repetitive brush pulling, we explored the woods along Mill Creek and skinny-dipped in deep spots in the creek. This didn't last very long because the creek water was cold (about 60 degrees F in the summer). One day as we were admiring the view from the trestle over Mill Creek, we heard the Shelton/Olympia lumber train coming. We ran and jumped off the tracks just ahead of the train and tumbled down towards the creek.

Watching the train pass was a daily highlight. One day we climbed the young alder trees along one side of the track to watch the top of the train. With the added weight, Gene's tree leaned over the tracks and he got a much closer view than he had planned. Fortunately the tree trunk cleared all parts of the train, but the branches Gene was clutching from the far side of the tree were whipped around by the passing freight cars. We did not try to get a top view of the train again.

Nearer home, we went swimming in Cranberry Creek in the pool formed behind the Castle's dam. The bottom was covered with about six inches of soft mud, which settled there from the winter floods. But the creek water was uncomfortably cold and the swimming lasted only a few minutes.

Two miles up the hill near Knutsens was an abandoned rotting log cabin near a small lake called Pigeon Roost Lake. Many years later the Boy Scouts developed one end of it as a summer camp and renamed it "Emerald Lake." In the late summer heat when the afternoon temperatures were above 90 degrees for a few weeks, the lake heated up to nearly 80 degrees. On some of these days, we hiked up to Pigeon Roost Lake. Arriving soaked in sweat, we stripped and splashed around for about an hour. The lake bottom was soft mud, which was crawling with salamanders. Feeling the wiggles and underfoot squirming added to the enjoyment. We then dressed and hiked home again, arriving soaked in sweat.

Coyotes could be heard howling in the woods at night. Abandoned dogs formed packs and sometimes joined in the evening chorus. One school recess, a dog pack chased several deer past the school grounds and into the Oakland Bay mud. The tide was out and the deer crossed the bay stepping high as the dogs bogged down in the deep mud. This provided the classes with their afternoon recess excitement.

Deer came down to Puget Sound regularly at night to lick the rocks and obtain a salt ration. Cow owners bought blocks of salt as a salt lick for the cows. These were pink and were etched into fanciful shapes by cow tongues.

Dad hand-sharpened the family knives and his crosscut saw. He acquired a grindstone formed by placing a pair of bicycle pedals vertically in a 15 inch round by two inch thick sand mold with one pedal buried in the bottom center then pouring several inches of concrete to fill the mold. When it set, it was a wheel with a bicycle axle through the center and pedals on both sides. This was mounted in a wooden frame with a seat so that the user could sit and hold his tool against the edge while he pedaled to turn the grindstone. Dad used this for initial tool grinding and a whetstone to put a fine edge on the knives and saws.

By late summer, the lush spring crop of field grass turns dry
and brown. Cow owners usually cut and store grass (hay)
in the late spring. After being cut fresh, the grass retains its
nutrients whereas the dead field grass does not.

One spring day, Dad bought a rusty old scythe and sharpened
it. He started cutting hay by hand in our field and traded off
with Gene and Leonard. By this painful process, and a month
of sporadic efforts, he managed to half fill the hayloft in the
barn. This provided marginally enough cow feed until the next
late fall grass crop had sprouted. In the following years, Dad
borrowed a horse and hay mower each spring and mowed
the field. He, Leonard, and Gene gathered the hay and stored
it in the barn. This provided more than enough summer hay
plus enough low-grade weeds to provide chicken house straw.
Many western Washington fields have scattered bracken ferns.
These were the source of most of the substitute chicken house
straw. He later bought bales of straw to soak up feces in the
barn and chicken house.

Dad had a moderately good baritone voice and sometimes
amused himself by singing as he drove the family around or
led a borrowed horse up or down the road to the highway.
He particularly liked civil war songs, Steven Foster songs of
the old south, and country and western songs. Several of the
neighborhood wives commented to Mom about how much
they enjoyed his singing and how lucky she was to have such

a cheerful husband! Those with other opinions about his singing did not pass them on to the Speece family.

The wood for the family stove was obtained from second growth fir trees, which had fallen during winters of heavy snow or ice storms (dead falls) at the edge of the family field. Dad and Leonard sawed these into 14-inch long logs, drove the pickup to the nearest spot in the field, tossed the logs in, and hauled them to a woodpile in the garage where they would later be split and stacked. If dead falls of an appropriate size (six to twenty inch diameter) were not available, they drove up an adjacent logging road until they found some in the logging scrap.

The young fir trees had numerous pitch blisters in the bark. After rainstorms we sometimes amused ourselves by scraping these off with our thumbnails and placing them as tiny boats in a mud puddle in the driveway. The water activated the pitch and caused the tiny boats to zip along leaving an oil-like rainbow colored wake. Mom did not approve because the pitch was very difficult to remove from clothing and children.

Until Neil's bed was moved upstairs in 1942, there were two old double beds with weak springs. Leonard had one and Gene and I shared the other. We were sound sleepers and moved very little during the night. After a few years, Leonard's bed had a dent in the middle, and the other bed had a dent on each side.

Barn swallows built mud nests along the eaves of the barn. Long skinny wasps we called mud daubers built similar mud homes along the eaves of the house. In the summer, we left the upstairs windows partly open for cooling. The windows had poorly fitting screens and the mud daubers frequently got into our bedroom.

We kept a fly swatter handy and created some morning excitement knocking things over as we chased them. There were also numerous spiders in the bedroom, but these were ignored. Many years later, when my half-grown kids visited the old homestead, my three daughters slept upstairs. The girls thought the mud daubers were interesting, but wanted me to assure them that all of the spiders and mud daubers in the room had been killed or removed before they would turn off the lights at night. We often amused ourselves in the morning with pillow fights. Sometimes a pillow split and scattered duck down all over the bedroom. This did not amuse Mom who had to clean up the messes around the house.

One morning we pawed through a trunk of old clothes. We found one of Mom's old red nightgowns. Leonard and Gene talked me into putting it on and climbing out the upstairs window over our enclosed porch. I ran down the porch roof to the garage roof and jumped off a corner while my older brothers laughed hysterically. Mom came upstairs to investigate the ruckus just in time to see me disappear off the garage roof. She ran downstairs, grabbed a broom, and chased me toward the barn. Beside the barn was an old rotting tree stump about ten feet tall. I scrambled up this, but lost my hold as the wood crumbled. The gown snagged near the top leaving my bare bottom dangling about six feet up. Mom gave it a few solid swats with the broom but by this time she was laughing too hard to be dangerous. She went back to the bedroom and gave each of my older brothers a few good swats also.

Each summer, Dad loaded the family into the old pickup a few times to drive to Allyn and visit his parents and sisters. We returned with apples, pears, and cherries from Linus' orchard.

As their youngest and most available child, Edith Kapalo was pampered by Linus and May. Jimmy and Daniel were frequent recipients of loose change to buy candy and comics. We liked to visit because that was our only chance to read comic books. The three Speece boys and the two Kapalo boys explored the surrounding area. In the forest was a 6x8x10 foot boulder apparently deposited there during the last ice age. We liked to climb around on this rock. Louie had a rowboat and we liked to row in the bay. One summer day, we had a jellyfish fight with a group of local boys in another rowboat. In the late summer, Puget Sound has many semi-transparent jellyfish up to several inches in diameter and very squishy. These were very effective in messing up clothes.

Nearly adjacent to our home was an old log cabin in a field. The Castles pastured horses in the field. One day as Leonard,

Gene, James Casteel and I were playing in the field, Leonard and James started throwing horse turds at Gene and me. We hid in the cabin and flung them back. We thoroughly plastered the cabin and ourselves. This did not amuse Mom, either.

A week after the horse turd fight, the Cochran family moved into the cabin and started fixing it up. The parents, Mary and Fred, had a son, Eddie, about Neil's age, and several daughters. Fred was crippled with polio, and Mary was friendly with several other local men to the point of going on overnight hunting and camping trips with them. In a few years, she divorced Fred and married one of these local men.

Across Cranberry Creek near the highway lived the Nason family. The father built a nice barn for the cows and chickens but the family house was a crude hovel with a dirt floor. They had several older sons and three daughters. The latter were in grade school with us. Leonard and Gene, with me trying to imitate them, were mean towards the Nason girls, the Cochran girls, and Lula. Doris was somewhat shielded by our parents from our crude behavior. I also bullied Neil and was ashamed of it through my adult years.

Several times the Kapalos visited our family. During these visits, various small items disappeared from our bedroom. One day Leonard couldn't find his pocketknife. I invited Danny to a wrestling match during which the knife and several other items fell out of his pockets.

With most of their children in school, Dad and Mom decided that the older ones should be assigned chores. In addition to chasing the two cows home each night, Leonard and Gene were assigned the chore of milking them. They were strongly discouraged from squirting each other, but couldn't resist aiming a few streams in the faces of the latest batch of kittens who waited expectantly during each milking. Mom had a one-gallon hand churn and assigned me the job of churning butter from cream she scooped from the top of some of the milk. Over time, a layer of cream forms at the top of a container of non-homogenized milk.

One summer morning, Mom decided to have each of us boys weed a row in the garden. Gene and I did a somewhat respectable job, but Leonard lay on the dirt groaning next to a ten-foot long row of newly sprouted carrots. Mom told him he could either do his weeding or lay there all day. He finally started inching himself along. Several hours later, he announced that he was done. He had pulled every carrot and left a neatly centered row of weeds.

One day I was standing on the landing near the top of the stairs examining the contents of boxes stored on the second floor. I pulled a box of canning jars towards me to get a better look. The box toppled off into my arms and I tumbled downstairs with it shattering jars on every step. I survived with hardly a scratch, but Mom reddened my rear end.

I enjoyed climbing trees. There was a large cedar tree by Cranberry Creek, which I particularly liked because from near the top I could see the bay, and Shelton in the distance.

Once when Leonard and Gene were chasing me, I climbed a several dozen-foot high fully branched fir tree with them close behind. From near the top, I slid down the outer branches past them to the ground.

One Christmas, Dad got each of us a BB gun (air rifle). The local birds and squirrels were never safe again. One day we were shooting tin cans off the tops of fence posts. As Leonard walked over to replace a tin can, I accidentally shot him in the shoulder. As Leonard charged me, I climbed a somewhat flimsy pair of vine maple trees. As Leonard started up after me, the two trunks pulled together on his hand. This hurt considerably more that the BB, but Gene talked Leonard out of killing his younger brother.

Each Easter, Mom hard-boiled two dozen eggs on Saturday morning. She helped us dye them in the afternoon, then packed them in a wicker basket. Dad and Mom got up early on Easter morning and hid them around the yard. Then Dad woke us up by yelling, "There's the Easter Bunny!" firing his rifle several times, and saying, "Dammit, I missed him!" We hurried out with an assortment of containers to hunt for the eggs. Mom helped the girls and Neil to make sure they got a few.

As we grew older, Dad hid the eggs one year along Cranberry Creek, and later in a section of old growth timber along Mason Lake. The purpose of the new locations was to have a greater variety of hiding places and a picnic after the event.

The Mason Lake area belonged to the Simpson Logging Company and was used by employees as a picnic area. It had a fresh water creek, Schumacher Creek, running into the lake and at the other end, Sherwood Creek running out to North Bay ten miles away in Allyn. Simpsons later installed a cookhouse and park equipment. In the early days of TV, they invited news commentator Arthur Godfrey to Shelton to gather material on the logging industry. They took him to the Mason Lake area and sawed down an old growth giant fir tree into the lake as part of their show for him.

One summer our family was picnicking at the Mason Lake area, and as we were swimming, Gene found an abandoned sunken rowboat. Leonard helped him get it floating and we jumped in and hand paddled it as Gene bailed vigorously with a coffee can. In a shallow spot, he quit bailing and announced that we were going to sink, but since he knew how to swim, he would get to shore to tell our parents where Leonard and I drowned. He then jumped over the side and swam to shore. Leonard noticed that we could easily wade to shore, but he started telling me to be brave and that we should drown like men. As I was wailing my last, the water flooded over the side of the boat and it settled to the bottom in two feet of water.

While we were still small, Dad acquired a camera. He lined all six of us up several times a year and took a picture. These had a staircase type feature in that we were lined up by age and each successively younger kid was three inches shorter.

Daymond and Mom

~ The War Years ~

In 1942, after the start of World War ll, the Simpson Logging Company started expanding the Shelton plant and hiring many of the unemployed people in Mason County. A new sawmill, plywood mill, and later a paperboard plant were added. The demand for lumber products mushroomed. Dad was hired and later trained as an electrician to help wire the new plants and keep the machinery running. Initially, he was in charge of using a small bulldozer to push sawdust from a large pile by the sawmill into the pulp and paper plant. Once the bulldozer rolled over in the soft sawdust pile, but its metal cover protected Dad.

By 1943, jobs were plentiful again. Ira Casteel got a job at the sawmill as a machinist (making and grinding metal parts). Louis Kapalo got a job in a logging camp helping haul logs and load logging trucks. Families started receiving presents other than necessities. At Christmas and for birthdays, the kids got gifts as well as clothes. With his new electrical training, Dad had electric wires strung on new poles from our nearest neighbors, who had electricity by late "39", to a distribution transformer beside our house. The Public Utility District paid for most of this. But Dad wired the house, installed electric lights, and connected us to the utility transformer. He also ran wires and installed lights in the barn and chicken house. He bought a radio and we started listening to various programs in the evening. After we diverted a stream through the cow pasture, Dad also erected a two-wire electric fence around it to keep the cows from wandering into the woods.

The Pope and Talbot Company, who owned the forests behind our home, logged the last of the local old growth fir forest, thus creating excellent wild blackberry picking for several years.

On some nights, Dad accompanied us upstairs and read us a Chapter from a book before turning out the lights. Dad liked Zane Gray novels so one of these was bought for me, since I liked to read novels, as Christmas and birthday presents each year. Later, I also got some Tarzan novels. Until 1942, most of the Christmas presents were clothes to replace those that wore out during the year.

Dad sold his old pickup truck and bought a second-hand Dodge sedan. The family started attending the Shelton Methodist Church every Sunday. Each kid was given a dime to put in the collection plate, and Dad and Mom each donated a dollar. We were told that the collection supported a Methodist missionary in China and helped feed the poor starving Chinese. I've since learned that at the time, the Japanese army was rapidly reducing the number of starving Chinese.

With his new vehicle, Dad started taking the family on Saturday summer outings and picnics. A favorite place was a public beach on Spencer Lake, two miles away, where we would all go wading and swimming.

For Christmas, Mom got a new dining table with eight wooden chairs and a refrigerator. We finally had a place to keep meat, milk, and fresh vegetables for a few weeks. The old family table became a picnic table in the yard, but it rapidly rotted away. Dad rented freezer space in Shelton for longer-term storage of meat that was mostly beef and venison plus salmon in the fall. Chickens were butchered one at a time as needed. Some of the extra salmon was smoked. Canned goods continued to be stored on shelves at one end of the porch. Mom also got an electric clothes washing machine with a hand roller wringer. But the outside clothesline still provided the final drying.

Dad purchased a gasoline engine powered drag saw for cutting wood. It weighed about 50 pounds and had hinged arms with short spikes (dogs) at the end. It was leaned across the log to be cut and the dogs were pounded in with a sledgehammer to hold it fixed. The engine would then be started by a battery powered ignition system and the crosscut saw blade would be dragged back and forth across the log until it was cut through. Dad would drive it in the back of the car to a deadfall, unload it, cut the tree into blocks of wood, load them and the saw into the back, drive them to the garage, unload them, split the wood, and store it in the garage. The drag saw often stayed outside with the dogs leaned back to either side until later use.

One day I was teasing Lula by called her "Toodie." Dad sometimes called her that. For some reason this nickname irritated her. She chased me around the garage and I jammed my knee into the upturned drag saw dog causing a bloody wound. Lula regarded this as adequate justice and Mom bandaged it up.

Mason County had a few scattered Japanese-American families who ran plant nurseries, stores, and other small businesses. We did not know any of them, and did not miss them when the government rounded them up and shipped them off to wartime camps. Their property was confiscated by neighbors. It was many years later before I realized the magnitude of this injustice.

Bremerton has a major US Naval base. In early 1942, the government decided to extend the Northern Pacific Railway spur from Shelton to Bremerton to provide a land route to ship heavy naval equipment to Bremerton. This was finished in a year and passed a mile up the hill from our place. The US navy also wanted a sea level canal dug from North Bay in Allyn through four miles of hills to the end of Hood Canal to provide an alternative route out of Puget Sound in case of a blockade by submarines or by the Japanese navy. At the time, the Japanese army occupied some of the Aleutian Islands off Alaska,. The Alcan Highway was nearly completed from Edmonton, Canada, to Fairbanks, Alaska. A Japanese mini-sub had surfaced near Ventura, California, and shelled an oil field and Japan launched a flock of incendiary bombs on helium balloons which were supposed to land in the west coast forests and explode on contact with the ground thus igniting massive forest fires (these started very few forest fires partly because most of them were launched during the west coast rainy season).

One day as we boys were walking down the railroad, we
rounded a curve to a quarter mile long straight stretch. Gene
told me that he bet he could carry me on his back to the next
curve. To me, this looked impossible so I agreed to bet. Gene
egged my bet up to a trillion gazillion dollars then carried me
down to the next curve. I never did pay off this bet.

One clear summer day a USAF P-38 fighter plane crashed
over the hill from our place. We heard the explosion as it hit
the ground and saw the pilot descending in a parachute.
We headed up the hill to try to find him but gave up and
came back as it got dark. Dad tuned in the evening news
on the radio, and determined that the crash was about four
miles away.

We all listened to the radio in the evenings. Dad's favorite
program was "Mr. President" which consisted of events
from a particular president's administration. The listeners
were expected to compete in identifying the president. We
also listened to the episodes of "The Shadow" and "Green
Hornet." I still remember the opening sounds of The Shadow.
These were a squeaking door slowly opening and an eerie
laugh followed by "Who knows what evil lurks in the hearts
of men? The Shadow knows"! In 1962, Lockheed, Sunnyvale,
wrote a computer program to compute the earth shadow
(eclipse) times for low earth military satellites. They called
it the "Lamont Cranston" program. The Shadow's name was

Lamont Cranston.

One of my favorite toys was a pot metal toy tractor with hard rubber tires. On rainy days, I liked to coast it out of the garage, which did not have a door, into the nearest puddle over and over. Another favorite toy was a tin propeller on a twisted metal strip. When pushed off, it spun up into the air for a few dozen feet, then coasted down again. Home made kites and thistle stalk bubble pipes were also popular. Mom would mix up hot soapy water cups for us. We loved to watch big soap bubbles float on the breeze.

When he was about six, Neil was playing in the dirt with Eddie Cochran when he threw his tin shovel down and said "This isn't any fun anymore. I wish I was young again".

One day, as I was perched on some boards overhead in the garage, the family dog wandered in. I called his name several times and he looked all around with a very puzzled look. Then I said "Look up." The dog immediately looked up and saw me. For a while, I was convinced that animals understood human speech but lacked the vocal chords to talk back.

Dad cut new fence posts and had us boys digging holes and helping him rebuild the pasture fences. There was an anthill in the way, so he placed a worn-out car tire around it, covered it with dry limbs, and set them on fire. The tire rubber caught fire and burned a hole in the ground where the anthill had been. Another time we stirred up an underground hornet's nest. Dad came back after dark with a flashlight, poured gasoline on it, and burned it out.

Mom wanted a picket fence around the house, so this was built with fir fence posts with poles between and five foot long by two-inch wide cedar pickets. She never liked it and it was eventually torn down and replaced with a hedge of bushes.

During the war years, Dad subscribed to Life Magazine which was filled with war pictures. The family went to several war movies in Shelton. These were gory attempts to inspire patriotism by depicting the Japanese as murderous slaughterers of innocents.

I became interested in jigsaw puzzles and got several with war themes as presents. One of my favorites was a German fighter plane being shot down during an American bombing raid. I had several nightmares of being bombed or shot by the Japanese. I had other nightmares of being pursued by wild animals that probably represented my two older brothers. These usually ended with me falling into a pit full of snakes and waking up.

It seemed that everything was rationed during the war. For the first time in years, Dad had money to spare. He finished paying for the house and starting paying $3500.00 for an additional five acres. But most consumer goods were rare.

Leonard and Gene pleaded with Dad to help them find a way to earn some money. The part-time man who had cleaned the

Oakland Bay School house each month now had a full time job and Lawrence Gosser arranged to have Leonard and Gene clean and polish the school floor at the end of each month for fifty cents apiece. I insisted on going with them so they let me help for free.

Amongst the alder trees near our home were numerous cascara trees. The tree bark can be peeled off, dried and processed into a powerful laxative. In the fall, the trees have potent berries. The Speece cows' diet included cascara leaves and, when they were present, the berries. The results reinforced the general feeling of thankfulness that cows don't fly. We got used to watching where we stepped as we walked across the field. The area behind the milking stalls was a perpetual soggy mess all year long. This was helped along by rain running off from Dad's add-on roof over the milking stalls.

In 1942 Dad showed us boys how to cut the live cascara tree bark with a pocketknife, peel it off and dry it. He then sold it in Shelton to provide us with another source of income. The following summer, he had Ira Casteel make three special purpose cascara peeling knives for us using scrap metal from the Simpson sawmill. The peeling killed the trees, but for a few years, the supply seemed inexhaustible. We cut down the taller tress before we peeled them. The dried bark sold for two cents a pound. We used the garage roof as a drying area. In several summers, Leonard earned enough to buy a bicycle, and Gene and I combined our earnings to buy a second bicycle. We peddled along the logging roads. Gene sometimes carried me on the cross bar of our bicycle in return for me pushing the bike up the steep hills. There was a lot of bicycle pushing on uphill slopes and a lot of coasting down hills.

One day we got all the way up to the Mason Lake Road on our bicycles. We were at the top of a steep hill down to the main highway by the bay. We decided to coast down the hill and ride home along the highway. Halfway down the hill in a high-speed coast, our chain fell off its sprocket and Gene aimed for a field beside the road and jumped off. The bicycle rolled end-over-end-over-me a few times before it stopped. The chain was reconnected and we rode the remaining one and a half miles home on level ground beside the main highway.

Near the end of the war in Europe, Roosevelt agreed to a Russian request that the other allied forces withdraw 60 miles all across Europe and cease fighting while Russia mopped up the German army and occupied Eastern Europe. At Yalta in 1945, after Roosevelt died, Truman asked Stalin to have Russia declare war on Japan to hasten the end of the Pacific war. Truman later declared that he really liked and trusted old Joe Stalin. Within weeks, the United States atom-bombed Hiroshima and Nagasaki, and Japan surrendered. Russia did not provide any physical support to the American forces, but occupied the Japanese Sakhalin Islands (the dragon's breath), and North Korea as part of the peace treaty. Berlin was within the Russian controlled area, but was jointly occupied by the United States, England, France, and Russia. Within a few years, Russia tried to force the other powers out of Berlin with a blockade, built the Berlin wall to prevent Germans from escaping from the Russian sector, and egged the North Koreans into a full-scale war to take over the American occupied south. The cold war was in full swing.

When the war finally ended in 1945, Dad bought Mom a new electric stove and refrigerator, and other appliances and Leonard and Gene each a 30-30 rifle. From that point on, they both skipped high school for two weeks during hunting season each fall to deer hunt with Dad and Ronnie Gosser.

One day as we were walking across the field, Leonard caught a garter snake. As he held it by the tail, he had an inspiration. He asked Gene and me to hold hands with him while he draped the snake over the electric fence. He explained that all of the electricity would go through the snake, but since it would split and we would each only get a third of it, we could watch the snake get electrocuted with almost no pain to us. Instead, the snake looked almost asleep and each electric pulse caused all three of us to jump together. After a few pulses, we killed the snake and decided to forget about electrocuting things.

~ The Early Teens ~

The war and rationing were over. The auto companies switched from jeeps and tanks back to cars. In 1946, the first few new cars since 1941 were sold to the public. Gas was no longer rationed nor travel restricted. Commercial rail and air travel were re-instated.

In 1946, Mom's dad came by train to visit for a week. Her mother died when she was twelve, and her dad died shortly after his visit. He did not show much interest in the Speece children.

With cigarettes no longer rationed, Dad started smoking again. One day as Leonard and Gene were watching him burn some trash, Leonard broke off a dry fern stem to about four inches long and lit the end to pretend that he was smoking. The fire raced up the dry stem and singed his nose. But within a few years, both Leonard and Gene were smoking when out of view of witnesses.

For evening recreation, Dad and Mom joined the Shelton Moose Lodge and began attending monthly meetings. Mom quickly decided that the purpose of the monthly meetings was to get drunk. After that Dad attended alone for a while, but took us boys to a movie during each meeting. Then the whole family started attending movies instead. Lula quickly became a fan of both Roy Rogers and Gene Autry (the singing cowboys) and decided she wanted to own a horse. She got a scrapbook for Christmas, and filled it with pictures of horses and movie cowboys. Most of the movies were reruns of war movies with, for example, John Wayne killing lots of Japanese soldiers. He got back to Indians in the next few years. After the war, many US movies were shown in Japan. In a poll, the Japanese were asked to name their most and least popular actors. The least popular was John Wayne and the most popular was "Gary, the Cooper".

One day, Dad showed us boys that he could wiggle his ears. This fascinated Leonard who practiced using various head muscles in front of a mirror until he finally found the right combination. He walked up to Dad and showed him his new found skill. Dad said, "Hell, any jackass can do that."

The Knutsens lived in a log house built by Buddy's dad and uncles. One day, Leonard proposed that we build a log fort by Cranberry Creek. We labored mightily to cut some fallen half foot thick alder trees into eight foot lengths with a crosscut saw, notch the ends with an ax, and assemble them into a boxy fort without doors or windows or a roof. It was about five feet high, and we entered through the open top. The cracks between the logs provided reasonable visibility from inside.

One fall day, Leonard and James Casteel caught a duck with a broken wing as it was feeding on a dead salmon. As James was trying to tame it, it shit on him and he wrung its neck. We started a fire and roasted the duck on an alder spit after removing its feathers, head, and guts. The pioneering spirit can only carry you so far. After the first bite of the partially raw rotten salmon flavored meat, we decided we didn't really need to be self-sufficient and went home to dinner. During this period, the Casteels were getting a divorce and their son, James, was living with us.

We frequently fished for trout in Cranberry Creek. We could usually dig up a few fish worms (angleworms) in the garden and use them for bait. Otherwise we caught crawdads in the creek, pulled off and skinned a chunk of white meat from the tail, and used it as bait. We threw the crawdad heads back into the creek. These attracted bullheads which were easy to catch using either crawdad tails or chopped up bullhead parts. We cut pieces of white meat out of each bullhead to augment our other bait. We usually caught a few six-to-eight inch trout, which we cleaned, and Mom fried for dinner. For fishing poles, we cut and trimmed willow poles and tied a fixed length of string with a hook on the end.

Gene was more patient than Leonard and me, and usually caught more fish. He also liked to fish by himself in Deer Creek along the swamp section. This was too brushy and log jammed to attract any other fishermen, and there were six-foot deep holes to wade through along with some swimming. This was easier than struggling through the brush, logs and stinging nettles along the shore. Gene usually caught half a dozen trout up to a foot long out of Deer Creek on each trip. The fish were transported by slipping a forked stick with a cut off branch through their gills and carrying the stick or tying it to his belt. The fishing technique included walking downstream while frequently kicking chunks of dirt from the bank into the water. This caused the trout to search the muddy water for fish worms, which Gene supplied as bait.

One day, Gene and I took Dad's sledgehammer along Cranberry Creek to smash rocks to see what was inside them. We found one rock with veins of gold. Gene took this one home and asked Dad what it was worth. Dad took it to a metal assayer in Shelton who told him with was worth less than the effort required to extract the gold. For years, Gene kept the rock in a secret hiding place in the barn loft. It was lost when the barn collapsed years later during a snowstorm.

Another time, Gene had me help him make a boat out of supermarket crates. We nailed two crates together end-to-end. We tore several other crates apart to get more sideboards to provide solid sides and bottoms. We smeared the ends of the slats with pine pitch to seal them against the wooden crate ends. Then we carried our creation to a deep spot in Deer Creek, got in, and pushed off. Our crack sealing job was somewhat imperfect since our weight bowed the bottom boards outwards and broke the seals. Our creation promptly sank and doused us. After observing the numerous leaks, we abandoned the project. The boat was left to float down Deer Creek, but we never heard of any sightings by neighbors or repeat experiments by other kids.

Dad had been a star of his high school baseball team, and

pitched for a year on a minor league team after high school. He hoped that his boys would be athletically inclined. He practiced softball with us. He put a basketball hoop on a pole in the yard and played basketball with us. He took the family to several Seattle Rainier baseball games. He offered to drive us to town if we would join intramural teams. But we developed few friendships with our classmates in Shelton. Following my older brother's lead some of the kids on the school bus liked to pick on me. Once I badly damaged my metal lunch box by bopping one of them over the head with it. In junior high, we tended to avoid our classmates at recesses. One day as the three of us were eating our lunches on the hilltop behind the school, some of the other boys started tossing rocks at us. This developed into a semi-serious rock fight. Fortunately, no one was hurt and it was not observed by or reported to any of the school officials.

To Dad's disappointment, none of his children showed much interest in sports or in becoming friendly with the school athletes. I was near the bottom of the pecking order in the gym class team selections. Our few friends were also not inclined towards competitive sports. The other Speece children were neutral towards the class athletes, but I actively disliked them because of their snide remarks on my lack of competitiveness.

Dad decided to encourage his boys to be more social by enrolling us in the Boy Scouts and becoming assistant scout leader. The troop met at a park in Shelton once a month and went on numerous overnight camping trips. Dad encouraged us to sign up for merit badge activities. Leonard and Gene both became moderately good at whip snapping. Gene applied this newfound skill to whip snapping garter snake heads off during camping trips. Once he whip-snapped a water snake with a large bulge below its head and a live frog flew out and hoped away minus most of its skin.

Once the troop was camped in a grassy area near Pigeon Roost Lake by an old partially collapsed log cabin with a log lined well nearby. The older boys discovered that the smallest boy in the troop was very scared of garter snakes, so four of the boys, one to each leg and arm, held him face up across the well while a fifth boy dangled a garter snake above his nose. The scoutmaster terminated this entertainment, but the boy dropped out of the scouts immediately afterwards.

The Mason County scout troops had a summer camp at a local lake. Us boys attended this for a week one summer. One day as we were playing in the lake, I stepped into an area that was over my head. As I was choking and sputtering, Gene dragged me back to a shallower area by the arm. Leonard learned to dog paddle at camp, but I didn't learn to swim until I was taught in a college gym class. Gene had taught himself to dog paddle much earlier in Pigeon Roost Lake.

All three of us won merit badges for knot tying, camping, and several other activities, but did not progress to any of the higher levels of scouting. The troop stars were the Hart brothers who were both Eagle Scouts. Their dad was the scoutmaster. The whole experience did not noticeably improve the social skills of the Speece boys. Neither did it make a serious dent in the Mason County garter snake population.

After the war, the Washington logging companies instituted reforestation in each logged off area. They had always left a few standing trees to provide natural reforestation, but now they actively planted small fir trees appropriately spaced across recently logged areas. The Simpson Logging Company also looked longingly at the old growth fir stands in Olympic National Park. The company supported a Shelton politician's run for the US Congress, and got him elected on a pledge to have the forest service open the South Olympics to logging (by Simpsons). This was done, and Simpsons extended their railroad into the area and built Camp Grisdale, a small city 40 miles from Shelton over gravel roads. Camp Grisdale provided room and board for the loggers and loading facilities for the railroad cars and logging trucks.

One of Dad's favorite Boy Scout camping areas was along the Wyanoochie River near Camp Grisdale. This area was "too wild" for the taste of the scout leader, particularly after Dad assured him that it was infested with bears and cougars (also known as pumas or mountain lions).

The congressionally stated purpose for logging in the national forests was to selectively remove sick trees and thin the forests. In viewing the denuded hillsides around Camp

Grisdale, I had to admire Simpsons approach to this goal.

In 1946, the Olympic elk herds had grown to where residents all around the South Olympic Park area were complaining loudly about bull elks molesting their cows during the fall elk-mating season. The herds had become nearly extinct in the early 20s from being hunted by mounted men with dog packs to supply eye teeth (two incisors) to the Elk Lodges for $1.00 apiece. In 1946, a hunting season was finally opened again, and Dad, Ronnie Gosser and my two older brothers had their first elk hunt. They quickly learned that the neck shots by the 30-30 rifles, favored for killing deer with minimum damage to the meat, did not stop the elk. The bullets simply balled up in the thick loose neck hair and caused bad bruises. The hunters quickly learned to aim for the head, and the elk learned to avoid the hunters. They were nearly tame at the start of the 1946 season.

For a week in the fall, the elk season overlapped the deer season and Gene and Leonard would both be "sick" and out of school that week.

One day our cousin, Chuck Cochrel, stopped to visit on his way back to Seattle after retiring from active overseas navy duty in Bremerton. He was a small muscular man who had won a bantamweight boxing title in the navy. He had two pairs of boxing gloves, and gave us boys a boxing lesson. Gene and Leonard tolerated this, but after a few minutes of being bopped in the nose, I started to cry. Chuck had also kept a military 30-06 rifle and some tracer shells. He fascinated us all by firing tracer shells into the woods at night to watch them ricochet from tree to tree. He also had a navy pack of bright green shark repellant dye (the green was to aid spotting by air search and rescue teams). He showed us boys what it looked like by dumping a packet in Cranberry Creek. This colored the creek and most of Oakland Bay bright green. Fortunately no concerned citizens were able to identify the source of it.

While dumping his dye in the creek, Chuck lit a cigarette and accidentally dropped his lighter in the pool, which was about five feet deep. Gene offered to retrieve it so he stripped to his shorts and Chuck held him by his ankles while he went in headfirst and picked it up.

Chuck went to work in Seattle, married a good Catholic Irish girl, Ginny, and raised a family. He liked to fish with Gene and visited on numerous weekends. A neighbor had stocked a trout pond, and Chuck quickly tired of Deer Creek swamp and learned to go there and catch a batch of large trout to impress Ginny with his fishing prowess.

In 1946, Uncle Louis Kapalo was standing next to a logging truck on a muddy road as a large bulldozer was being loaded on the bed. The truck wheels sank into the mud on the side next to Louis, and the bulldozer upset sideways on him. Edith and the boys and grandparents and Speece family all attended the funeral. We were flabbergasted at the way Jimmy and Daniel joked about their dad throughout the ceremony. In the mid-1970s, Jimmy Kapalo was killed in an almost identical logging accident.

~ The Oyster Beds ~

Lawrence Gosser was impressed by the conscientious job
Leonard and Gene did in cleaning the Oakland Bay School
House each month. In the summer of 1945, he hired Leonard
and Gene for fifty cents per hour apiece to work in his
oyster business.

Lawrence raised Japanese oysters on the gravel beaches of
Harstine Island. These oysters are much larger than the badly
depleted native Puget Sound oysters, but they do not spawn
readily in the cold waters of Puget Sound. Lawrence had
discovered that they will spawn in the warmer water at the
muddy end of Hood Canal, but if left there, they sank into the
deep soft mud and grew very long and skinny (to keep their
tips out of the mud).

Lawrence leased and later bought land at the end of Hood
Canal and along Harstine Island. He had an oyster shelling
and canning area next to his home at the end of Oakland Bay.
He built a large float (water-filled scow-like device) to dump
the oysters in prior to shelling. His wife, Elinor, worked with
him and became an expert oyster sheller (shucker).

Lawrence had Leonard and Gene (and later, me) help load
oysters at Hood Canal into apple boxes and sturdy crates he
had built. They wore hip boots and leather vests and gloves.
The boxes were stacked on a barge resting in the mud. This
was done at low tide. As the tide rose, the barge was towed up

to a more solid part of the beach where Lawrence parked an old truck with wooden side rails. This was loaded up with the crates full of young oysters and chains were strapped across the back. Lawrence loaded Elinor and their sons in front and had us sit on top of the back row of oyster crates and hang onto the top chains while he drove 15 miles to the Harstine Island Ferry Landing. His arrival was timed to be just ahead of a scheduled ferry departure. We rode the ferry across Pickering Passage and rode another few miles to his Harstine Island beach. Here, the tides were several hours later than in Hood Canal, and the gravel beaches were solid enough to drive the truck down nearer the water. Lawrence had a heavy farm tractor with cleated steel tires and a makeshift flatbed trailer. The oyster boxes were loaded on the trailer and hauled along the waters edge where they were dumped. If the tide was too far in, the crates were loaded on a barge and dumped out in the desired area. Oysters and clams thrive in the part of the bay that is above the low tide level, but are under water when the tide reaches its mean level between low and high tide.

Lawrence only paid Leonard and Gene for the time when they were picking up or dumping oysters. The truck rides were on their own time. Their work hours varied with the tides from before daylight in the morning until late afternoon. Some of the oyster loads were picked up from the fattened oysters on Harstine Island and hauled to his opening house and dumped in his float in Oakland Bay.

My brothers got used to Lawrence's nearly continuous

exhortations, "Hurry, boys, hurry, the tides a coming!" but they worked enough hours to accumulate some savings. Gene bought a 30-06 army surplus rifle and found that it had enough power to kill an elk with a neck shot.

Lawrence was pleased with his hired help and asked the boys if they knew someone else who could work on the oyster beds. At their recommendation, he also hired Buddy Knutsen the following summer.

The oyster business had become very profitable, and Lawrence acquired an abandoned homestead on 20 acres of grassy hillside with scattered maple trees at the end of Oakland Bay across from his home and oyster house. He cut down and burned the trees, planted an apple orchard, and built a new two-story house, which the family moved into in late summer 1946. The previous fall, his oldest son, Larry, had started grade school in Oakland Bay School only one-quarter mile away but two miles from the old home across the bay.

In early June when Lawrence hired my brothers for the summer oyster business, he was burning the fallen maple trees with the help of a large lighter fluid squirt gun. He was trying to keep six different fires going on the hillside.

One morning about 8:00, I walked to Lawrence's new place with Leonard and Gene. He asked them to meet him there for the drive to his Hood Canal seed oyster bed. He had just started his maple tree fires. I pleaded with him to let me work for the day with Leonard, Gene, and Buddy Knutsen who had also walked from home. Instead, he handed me his squirt gun and asked me to keep his fires burning until I got tired, then put the squirt gun away and go home. He said he would pay me $.25 an hour for however long I worked. Then he loaded the other boys in the back of his truck on top of empty oyster boxes (which looked very much like apple boxes, including a few surviving labels), loaded Elinor and his boys, Larry and John, in the front seat and left for Hood Canal 17 miles away.

That evening Leonard and Gene got home about 7:00 pm and Mom asked, "Where's Daymond?" She phoned Lawrence who drove to his new place and found me still tending fires at 8:00pm. After considerable grumbling, he paid me $4.00 and drove me home. Shortly after that, he hired me on his oystering crew at $.50 an hour.

That fall, the Harstine Island starfish population increased markedly. Oysters have two major predators: starfish and sea snails. The local starfish were five armed and about eight inches from arm tip to arm tip. They wrap their arms around a clam or oyster, and pull the shell until the oyster muscle gets tired and the shell pulls open. They push their center (stomach) into the shell and eat (dissolve) the oyster. The Puget Sound sea snails are about an inch or two in diameter. They attach themselves to the shell like a barnacle and excrete an acid, which eats a hole in the shell. Then they extend their stomach through the hole to eat the oyster or clam.

On very low tide days, Lawrence took us to Harstine Island
and had us hand him each starfish we could find. He cut
each one into about a dozen pieces with a pair of tin snips
and tossed them back in the bay as fish and crab food. The
fish didn't like them. The crabs got a few pieces, but most
of the pieces grew into whole new starfish. After a few loud
profanities, Lawrence made a new attack. He drove his tractor
and trailer along the low tide water edge and had us toss all
the starfish we could find onto the flat bed trailer. He hauled
several loads of them to a clear spot just off the beach and
dumped them in a pile which became a mound about six feet
in diameter and two feet deep. About a week later, the pile
reached maximum odor, and we all kept as far away from it
as possible.

Another oysterman told Lawrence that you could kill starfish
by jabbing them in the head with a salt dispensing spear.
Lawrence rigged up a spear and found that this actually
worked. After that, he kept his spear loaded and next to him
in his tractor and killed any starfish he found on his beaches.
The sea snails were never plentiful and did not constitute a
similar problem.

On the way back from Harstine Island, we stopped several
times to visit with Elinor's parents, the Jones, who lived in
a large house near the ferry landing. Whenever Lawrence
started to tell them about a problem, Mrs. Jones would say, "If

it isn't one,thing, it's twoooooo." Elinor had Lawrence hire her brother, Keith, when he was between other jobs, which was most of the time. He was a friendly, jovial man and presented quite a contrast to Lawrence's all business attitude.

We found that there were octopuses in Hood Canal, but they were small and not at all dangerous looking. We also found that a few of the oysters had pearls, but they were small and dull colored. Lawrence tried to sell some and was told that they were worthless.

With us boys earning money from Lawrence, Doris and Lula started taking local babysitting jobs. Doris was more aggressive than Lula, and became a regular baby sitter for the Taylors who owned a ranch between where Cranberry Creek and Deer Creek empty into Oakland Bay. They later named this "The Two Rivers Ranch".

As Lawrence's boys, John and Larry, grew older, he assigned more and more oyster bed chores to them. They both grew up hating the oyster business and moved east after they graduated from college. John earned a BA in psychology, and Larry earned a PhD in chemistry. Larry loved hiking and rock climbing, and moved back to Port Angeles at the north end of the Olympic Mountains after he retired from an oil company in New Jersey. After Elinor's parents and Keith and her sister died, she became very active with her remaining in-laws to the extent that Lawrence felt ignored and divorced her and moved to Olympia. The oyster business had shut down earlier after Larry and John both graduated from college and refused to support it. After Dad died, Elinor also visited a lot with our Mother.

Daymond and cow

~ Old Hoss Duke ~

In the spring of 1945, Dad decided to buy a horse to plow and cultivate the garden, pull logs out of the woods, and help with numerous hauling jobs. He built a horse stall in the barn, and bought a harness, plow, and some cables. The horse was a sway backed old beast named Duke. We had already spread chicken manure on the garden area, and Dad and Duke started plowing it. It was a pretty erratic job. Duke wasn't into steady pulling. Each time Dad whacked him in the rear with the harness straps, he would leap ahead, then stop. If Dad had the plow aimed up slightly, it would jerk out of the ground. If aimed down, it would dig in and Duke would sometimes jerk Dad over the top of it by the reins. Dad tied the reins around his chest so that he could steer Duke by twisting his chest while guiding the plow with both hands.

After lots of jerks and profanity, the garden was finally plowed. Hauling logs for firewood was an equally jerky operation. Duke quickly learned that if he fell down on his side after a big jerk, he might be unharnessed to allow him to get up again after which he would run back to the barn. Leonard was usually asked to carry the harness back.

Dad's Dodge didn't start readily in cold weather, and the next winter he often harnessed up old Duke and got Leonard up to help get the Dodge pulled until it started. After the first time the headlights were never again pointed in the same direction. Dad sat in the car working the choke, ignition, and throttle while Leonard had Duke try to pull. After each mighty jerk, the car bumped Duke in the rear, and he partially sat down on the headlights. Yet somehow, the car would get started and Dad leave for work while Leonard unharnessed Duke and put him back in the barn, and had breakfast with the rest of us.

The water from the porch pump got rustier each year, and Dad decided during the war to haul Cranberry Creek water for cooking and drinking. He got a 100 gallon used oil drum in Shelton, steam cleaned it, had Ira cut off the top with an acetylene torch, and built a sturdy sled. He towed this sled and barrel to Cranberry Creek, and bailed it full with a water bucket. When he tried to tow it home with the Dodge, he found that he had to dump most of the water back in to the creek before he could move it. The Dodge was heavy but still couldn't move the sled and the full barrel out of the creek gravel. Duke did much better than cars at towing the family water. His mighty jerks were not sufficient to upset the barrel.

Eventually, I was assigned the job of refilling and hauling the family water barrel. Once when Old Duke jerked, I fell down in front of the sled. The next jerk pulled it over my legs. But Duke wasn't being whopped in the rear, so fortunately he stopped long enough for me to extricate myself.

Dad taught Leonard how to harness Duke. But Duke could see that Leonard had some difficulty in getting the harness over his back. Early on, he found that if he put a hoof on Leonard's foot, he could foil the process. As he held Leonard's foot down, he turned his head and bit Leonard on the shoulder. One day, he tried this on Dad, who grabbed an available 2x4 about three feet long, and nearly floored old Duke with a whack across the forehead. After that Leonard kept a 2x4 club handy and after a few applications, Duke didn't step on his foot anymore either.

Dad got a cultivator and started using Duke to cultivate between the garden rows to keep the weeds down. We had parallel rows of pea vines growing on a six-foot high chicken wire fence. Whenever Dad started down these rows, Duke grabbed a mouthful of peas from whichever side he could reach first. Dad jerked the reins to pull his head away from that side, and Duke grabbed a bite from the other side. Dad eventually gave up on using Duke to cultivate the peas or corn, which Duke also savored.

On the first day of elk hunting season in 1946, Dad's hunting party, which included Gene, Leonard, and Ronnie Gosser, killed several elk across the Satsop River about a mile off the Camp Grisdale Road. They cleaned the elk and started to pack them out but quickly limited themselves to one quarter of one elk apiece. They were all worn out when they got back to the car, and Dad said "let's borrow a truck and bring Duke back to pack out the other one tomorrow." So they did. But when Duke started up the narrow trail from the river, he fell over sideways and wedged the elk under him against a tree on the drop off from the trail. With mighty efforts, the hunters got him unharnessed and back on his feet. He ran back to the truck while they packed the second elk and his harness back.

Dad bought an old buckboard carriage in town and towed it home. He hitched up old Duke and amused Mom with a horse and buggy ride through the neighborhood. Then he turned the carriage over to us boys. We had all developed sore bottoms from bareback riding but now we thought we were really in style.

One sunny day, we hitched Duke to our carriage and rode up the logging roads to the hilltop above Deer Creek and around to the road back home nearer Cranberry Creek. The logging company had stretched a cable across the road at the top of the hill to keep people out and thus reduce the risk of forest fires. Leonard told Gene and me that since he was in charge of driving Duke, we would have to get off and lift the buggy wheels over the cable. So he stepped Duke over it and we lifted the front and got those wheels over it. When we lifted the back wheels over the cable, the buggy lurched forward and bumped Duke in the rear. He took off at a gallop down the steep gravel road. As they zipped around a corner at the bottom, a front wheel hit the end of a log. The buggy and Leonard were airborne for a few feet and landed separately. Duke galloped home with the damaged buggy as we dashed down the hill to help Leonard. With a sprained ankle, he limped home with us. That was our last long buggy ride.

After two years, Dad decided that he'd had enough of Duke. Leonard helped load him up and haul him off to a local fox farm. After Dad collected a nominal fee for fox food and shot Duke, they came home again. Leonard proclaimed that the happiest day of his life. But for years afterwards, Leonard would tell friends how amusing it was to watch Dad plow with Duke. He vividly described old Duke jerking Dad over the plow and dragging him face down through the garden splattering rooster tails of chicken manure to either side of his nose.

The buggy was parked in our field near Cranberry Creek for a while. There was a hill down towards the house. We would push it up the hill then jump in and coast down again. One day Jimmy and Daniel Kapalo were helping us. Leonard had Jimmy stand in front holding the buggy as the rest of us jumped in. With the extra weight, it pushed Jimmy over backwards and coasted over him and down the hill. Eventually Dad sold it to a buggy collector for more than he had paid for it.

~ The DayGene Canal ~

About a quarter-mile into the woods beyond our field is a small stream that flows about a half-mile from a peat bog into Cranberry Creek. When the railroad was built, it partially dammed the bog thus increasing the water level and summer flow of the stream which was supplied by swamp water which had seeped through gravel for several dozen feet to emerge in the creek canyon.

In the fall of 1945, Dad decided to divert the creek down to our field and have a more convenient source of water for the cows and us. He dug a new channel for several hundred feet then blocked the old channel. The water rushed into the new channel and disappeared down the mountain beaver holes, and under the tree roots within a few dozen yards. Dad kept digging and filling beaver holes but after a few weekends, he became disillusioned at the thought of how far he had to ditch it to get it to our field. By this time, Gene and I got enthusiastic and worked the ditch a few hundred more feet to the old skid road that had a gravel bed. We found that the water drained away more slowly through the packed gravel bed of the old skid road. And the muddy late fall flow with some help from us was sealing the drainage paths. By Thanksgiving, we had a trickle of water flowing into our field. We convinced ourselves that a muddy winter flood would seal the leakage paths and provide a steady flow by the following summer. Having done most of the work, we named our waterway the DayGene Canal.

Mountain beavers are muskrat sized rodents that live on roots and dig underground burrows. These later become homes to skunks, weasels, and other varmints. They have also accounted for quite a few broken legs of horses being galloped through the woods.

In the fall, trout swim up small side streams from the creeks looking for worms washed from the banks as the rainy season floods increase. By January 1946, our diverted creek was at flood stage and had formed a large pool several inches deep at a low spot in our field. Then the rains quit for a while and we had a deep freeze. One day as I was walking across the ice over this pond, I saw several large trout swimming under the ice. When they tried to return to Cranberry Creek, they ended up in our field. I got my Dad's 22-rifle, and walked across the ice to each trout I could see. I aimed straight down at each one's head and fired. Then I reached through the resultant hole and pulled out a trout. I got nearly a dozen 8 to 12 inch trout this way. It was by far my most successful trout catching afternoon.

There was an abandoned well at a low spot at the edge of our property line. The spring floods down through our field from the diverted stream nearly filled it with silt. But it took several winter floods to silt up the new DayGene Canal bed through the woods enough that the stream ran through our field all summer. By then, Dad had dug a roughly 5 by 5 by 5 foot square hole in its path at the upper end of the field, lined it with concrete blocks, built a pump house over it, installed a pump and electric wires, and helped us boys dig trenches and lay pipe to the house. We now had running water in the house and for watering the garden, although it had a murky brown color during the rainy season. We dug a hole in the stream bed below the pump house and installed an old leaky clothes washing tub to form a half-foot deep drinking spot for the cows. As a bonus for the cows, the field grass along the steam stayed lush and green all summer.

Given a reliable water supply, Dad had us help build a new electric fence around the field. It had two strands of wire and pulsed every few seconds. This kept the cows in the field away from the cascara trees and out where they were easy to find. Each of us boys learned the hard way not to grab the top wire when climbing over it and not to pee on it.

The little canal was a reliable source of water for years, but was eventually replaced by a deep-water well which provided clean year round water. The plumbing from the well pump was connected to the old galvanized underground pipe system from the abandoned pump house.

Dad was not alone in trying to access water from year around streams. Ira Casteel got many sections of wooden pipe at a bargain price and used it to run a stream from a hill on the far side of Deer Creek into his yard. Dick Fox, a loner who lived on Ira's property, nailed planks together in a V-shaped trough to carry water from a stream across Deer Creek to his yard (he lived in a one-room cabin he had built) to provide year around watering of a colorful flower garden, which he developed and maintained.

~ *High School* ~

I started high school in September 1947, a year behind Leonard and Gene. The teachers were pleased that I seemed to be a serious student in contrast to my older brothers. Their class had a bad reputation for rowdiness. Our ancient English teacher, Mrs. Cecilia Bell, had false teeth, a wig, and a pompous manner. The boys snorted and shot spit wads at her when she was facing the blackboard until either a plate or a wig would sometimes come loose or she would throw an eraser at one of them. One class assignment was to write a paper on some phase of Shakespeare's life. Leonard was asked to read his to the class. To her annoyance, it was all about the family chamber pot and its contents, which the bard dumped out their second story window each morning.

We each took typing class. Gene took unkindly to uncooperative machinery and often expressed his opinion to his typewriter. The teacher reprimanded him frequently and told him that it was pointless and infantile to cuss at an inanimate object.

Leonard and Gene took a senior year auto repair class. The previous year, Dad got Leonard a Model A Ford, then a year later, got Gene one. At the time, the Shelton High School required that each senior take some career-training course. For the girls, it was usually home economics. I took carpentry. I also took a high school driving class, and Dad got me a nondescript car for $35 when I graduated. It was a rusty 1933

Ford with a 1938 Mercury V8 engine welded into it.

I thoroughly examined my car and noticed that the brake linings were rusty. After I oiled them, it had no brakes. One day I took Jimmy and Daniel Kapalo for a drive. Half way up a hill I tried to shift into second gear and couldn't get it back in gear. It coasted backwards down the hill where I veered off the road and knocked down a sturdy willow tree over an old fir stump. The car slid up the willow tree and stopped with both rear tires off the ground. It was not damaged but the three of us couldn't slide it off the tree so I went to the nearest house and borrowed an ax. When I got back and as I was cutting the willow tree in two, my cousins were peeling (and killing) nearby cascara trees. When the willow tree was cut in two, the rear wheels dropped to the ground and I drove back onto the side of the road. As I returned the ax my cousins loaded up their cascara bark and we drove home. Dad asked where the bark came from, and when I told him, he bawled me out for letting them destroy someone else's property.

Leonard loved his car, and we rode it to school nearly every day instead of the bus. He parked it near our back door. The out-house was about 50 feet beyond it. Initially, at natures call, he would jump in his car and drive to the out-house, then back when he was done. It was our usual transportation to and from school; Gene viewed his car as transportation too and complained that it seemed to have a top speed of 45 mph. The first time he drove Dad to town, Dad cautioned him to slow down on the curves to which Gene said, "Hell, even the fish worms are passing us at this speed!"

Leonard overhauled his car engine. Our garage had a sturdy beam across the entry to which he fastened Dad's 1000 pound test come-along (a cable and pulley device). He drove the car under this, unbolted the engine, bolted it to the come-along cables, and pulled it into the air. He pushed the car out from under it until he was done working on the engine. There was occasional profanity as his tools slipped and he skinned his knuckles.

When Leonard was done, Gene gave his car engine the same treatment. Near dark, his wrench slipped and he badly skinned one knuckle. With loud profanity, he hurled most of his tools out into the weeds. The next morning he allowed that it wasn't their fault and I helped him find them again.

One day, several boys showed up at school with a Model T Ford, which they had retrofitted with a Mercury V-8 engine. They were bragging about how fast it would take off. To show the gathered crowd, they revved the engine, let out the clutch, and jerked ahead several feet as the wooden spokes splintered and shot out of both rear wheels. The rapidly spinning rear axle dropped onto the rims.

Donny Gosser dropped out of junior high school in about the eighth grade. After he bummed around for a while, his dad told him to go hang around me and absorb some inspiration. That summer, to Dad's disapproval, he visited me several times. I advised him to go back and finish school. He tried, but gave up again. That was my last contact with him. His younger brother, Eddie, didn't finish school either.

Some of the Allyn kids went to the Shelton High School. One day, Bob Eldrich, who was in my class, and Jimmy Kapalo were amusing themselves by lighting matches and holding them over the fumes from an empty 500-gallon oil drum that they were leaning on. Suddenly the fire ran into the barrel and the fumes exploded. The bottom bowed out and the barrel shot several feet into the air tearing off Bob Eldrich's left arm and badly scarring Jimmy's right arm.

One of the Allyn kids in Gene and Leonard's class commented on how the Speece kids were a bunch of wimps. One recess, the other kids egged him into starting a boxing bout with Leonard. After some amateurish posturing and jabbing, Leonard bopped him in the nose. At that point, he called it off. He said "I can't box with him! He has the reach on me."

As soon as war surplus vehicles hit the market, Dad traded in his old Dodge for an army surplus canvas roofed command car (oversized jeep). After the war, we faithfully attended the Methodist Church in Shelton. On the way home, I usually tried to read the handouts and arrived home car sick. One summer day, I was berating my brothers about something when a yellow jacket (wasp) blew in the window and into my mouth. It stung me twice on the way down my throat. I didn't need any emergency treatment, which shows that I was very lucky and am not allergic to yellow jacket stings. My brothers attributed this incident to a silent request to the powers that be to get me to shut up.

Miss Hawthorne was our math teacher. She was our youngest teacher and I thought she was beautiful. One day, when she was out of the room, the other boys egged me into jumping out our second story classroom window. I landed in a muddy flowerbed, and got back after Miss Hawthorne. She gave me a curious look but didn't ask where I'd been or why I was tracking mud into her classroom. Someone might have told her I jumped out the window.

I was always picked last for sports teams and ignored during most of the play. In one football game, the quarterback passed the ball to me because no one was guarding me. I trotted through the opposite team players, who ignored me as they tried to find the ball. We were near our own goal post, but as I ambled down the field, the word got out that I had the ball. At a fast walk, I would have made a touchdown, but one of the opposing players tagged me out near their goal line after a long chase. That was the closest I came to scoring in any school game.

A family friend encouraged me to join a 4-H Club. I exhibited a wooden toolbox at the Mason County Fair and won a blue ribbon. The next year, I won a variety of ribbons by displaying vegetables from the family garden. The 4-H Club was my first organized activity where I was not one of the youngest members. It was a real morale booster.

That summer, the state 4-H Association sponsored a trip to Washington State Agricultural School near the Idaho border. We took a train both ways. It was an exciting new experience for me. We got to talk briefly on a radio show at the college. I particularly remembered a cow with a hole cut from her side into her stomach and enclosed with a glass plate through which you could watch the food churning in her stomach.

A usual biology class activity was to amass and label leaf collections. Showing glued together small animal skeletons was also encouraged. Gene shot a squirrel with Dad's 22 rifle, boiled the bones clean, and glued them together for his exhibit. As he was explaining some missing (shot away) bone parts, the class broke into noisy laughter and the class was dismissed.

The high school had a glee club which Leonard, and Gene joined. So our family attended several evening sing fests. I loved their renditions of "the Bells of Saint Mary's" and "The Tree in the Meadow".

One of my classmates was fascinated by logging trucks and spent hours drawing detailed pictures of them down to the tire bolts. As a result he never heard anything the teacher said.

In 1949, Western Washington had a large afternoon earthquake, which cracked the State Capitol dome in Olympia. It was between classes at Irene S. Reed High School and the stairway to the second floor was crowded. I was at the bottom when I felt the shaking. I looked back and saw a screeching crowd swaying with the stairway. I thought it was the students shaking the building by rocking in unison until it was announced that we had an earthquake. One girl fainted.

As the class of "49" neared graduation, Dad started querying Leonard and Gene about college plans and career plans. They both told him that they planned on doing better than he had without going to college. When he asked me the same questions a year later, I said I wanted to be a doctor and a missionary, and go heal all the poor starving people in Africa. Dad scowled and said I probably couldn't get into medical school because my father wasn't a doctor, and besides, it's an 8-year course, and he couldn't afford to help me much. He asked for a second choice. I said I'd like to be a lawyer and represent all the poor people who couldn't afford lawyers. He scowled again and asked if I was interested in any 4-year courses. I told him I might like electrical engineering because it required lots of math and the University of Washington brochures said that it was their toughest four-year course. He smiled, patted me on the back, and congratulated me on a good choice.

~ Our Grandparents Move In ~

After Uncle Louis died, Edith and the kids moved to Wenachee in central Washington where she drove a taxi to help support them. Linus and May were in their late 80s and Dad worried about their ability to take care of themselves. In 1946 he talked Mom and them into selling their Allyn home and moving in with us. He started building them a one-room cabin about 100 feet from our house and moved in some of their appliances and property. The cabin was never finished. It became another family storage building and provided a dry place for the squirrels to scatter pinecones around above a paperboard-enclosed ceiling. Their bed was temporarily located in our living room until Dad moved them into a rest home where they died in the mid 50s.

Grandpa spent his afternoons snoozing in a rocking chair in the living room. As he fell asleep, he would breathe more and more slowly and deeply until he woke himself up again with a great gasp of breath. This pattern results from a sometimes life threatening condition called "sleep apnea." He told Mom that he enjoyed his naps but the snorts between the naps were wearing him out.

Grandma loved to wander in the woods but she had Alzheimer's disease and frequently got lost. Finding her several times a week became one more of our chores.

Grandma loved to tell us about her childhood adventures in

Minnesota. She told us her local area had dangerous hoop snakes. These are large poisonous snakes that frequently attacked members of her grade school. One day as she was walking home from school, she saw one eyeing her from a hilltop. As it grabbed its tail in its mouth and started rolling down the hill towards her, she hid behind a tree. As it rolled rapidly towards the far side of the tree, it uncoiled and sunk its fangs into the tree. Before it could pull them loose, she ran home. The next day, she noticed that all the leaves had fallen off the tree and it was dead.

When Mom didn't wash the dishes right after a meal, Grandma would do it. She would fill a dirty glass with cold water, shake it around, pour it into the next glass, and repeat until the glasses were done. Then she would dampen a washrag in the final glass, wash a plate or utensil, rinse the rag in the same glass, and repeat until all the dishes were "washed." After they were mounted in an air-drying container she would throw out the last of her glass of water. After she left, Mom would rewash the dishes in a basin of soapy hot water, rinse them in a basin of clean hot water, dry them with a dishtowel, and put them away. We asked Grandma why she didn't use more water to wash the dishes. She said that would be wasteful and her Mom taught her to save water during the great 1870s droughts in Minnesota when whole towns died of thirst.

In my early teens, I became fond of jigsaw picture puzzles and received a new one for each Christmas and birthday. When

Grandma saw me working on one, she would always help me. Her sight was very poor, but she would steadily pound pieces into places where they almost fit. I would give up after a while and we would both leave. After she was out of sight, I would come back and remove a bunch of miss-fit pieces, then continue with the puzzle.

In the summer of 1949, Dad had accumulated three weeks of vacation beyond hunting season requirements, and decided to use it on a vacation to Ohio with Mom to visit with their brothers, sisters, and families. As a comfortable car full, he took the girls and Neil along. He told us older boys that we should continue doing our chores and that Grandma would cook for us.

By 1949, I had become very interested in religion and started reading the Old Testament cover to cover. I was bothered by the discrepancy between our Sunday school description of a merciful god who loved children and all people, and a god who destroyed the cities of Sodom and Gomorrah, men, women and children, because the inhabitants annoyed him. He also destroyed many other people and armies because they mistreated his chosen people, the Jews. I wondered if any of us had a chance of going to heaven since we weren't Jews.

After three days of Grandma's cooking, my older brothers collared me and told me that I was going to be the cook and that reading the bible wasn't going to save my soul if we all died of food poisoning. I objected that I didn't know anything about cooking. They told me that neither did Grandma and that I could read the cookbook, and that I might die soon if I didn't get off my butt and start cooking. So, over Grandma's objections and everyone else's blessings, I became the cook.

Initially, I only broiled and served carrots, peas, potatoes, and meat in separate containers. I mashed the potatoes and served them with gravy from the meat. Grandma looked at my first lumpy partially mashed potatoes and told me that I should have asked for her help with the dumplings. But my brothers wanted more variety, so I started heating up canned corn, and beans, serving canned fruit, and frying steaks. Then they asked for a pie. A neighbor had donated some fresh cherries, so I tried to make a cherry pie. I thought I had followed the cookbook directions, but it came out of the oven with a very skimpy crust and with the cherries floating in a thin syrupy liquid. I got to eat it all by myself.

We were all having cold cereal with milk and sugar for breakfast and making our own peanut butter and jelly sandwiches for lunch, so dinner was my only meal responsibility. Some stuff was ripening in the garden, so we also had lettuce and tomatoes for tossed salads. One day, Gene picked several buckets full of cucumbers, collared me and announced that we were going to can some pickles. We spent an afternoon slicing them, putting them in canning jars with our own brine mixture, and sealing and boiling them. We saved a small bowl of raw slices for me to use in dinner salads. At one point, I got careless and the end of my thumb ended up in one of the jars. We put about a dozen quart-jars of them on a pantry shelf and declared it a job well done.

It was a frubious day for the whole family when our parents got home. I swore I would never cook again. After we all told our adventure stories, Mom examined our pickles. We later caught her dumping the whole endeavor and washing the jars. Our special chores were once again reduced to finding Grandma each time she got lost in the woods.

~ The Fur Trade ~

About 1948, a neighbor donated a pair of white rabbits to Dad who first determined that Leonard was agreeable to raising rabbits for fur and meat. Dad helped him build three rabbit feed cages. They were three feet by three feet by two feet high boxes on four-foot legs planted in the ground. Each box had a roof and three wooden sides, but the door facing out and the bottom were of about half inch by half-inch wire mesh. That way there was a box for older rabbits or males, a box for younger rabbits or females, and a box for new mamas. The pee and dobbles would drop out the bottom. Each cage had a food dish and a water dish.

When Leonard started off happily breeding his initial two rabbits, Gene bought several steel traps and announced that he was going to trap mink along Cranberry Creek. He invited me to join him, so he would have company as he checked his trap line. We started out setting traps in holes along Cranberry Creek, which were mostly old mountain beaver holes. The mountain beaver is a rodent about the size of a large rat. They dig holes all over the wooded areas in the northwest, which are later used as homes by weasels, skunks, and other varmints.

We set our traps, placed them out of sight inside the holes, drove sharpened foot long wooden spikes through the rings at the ends of the chains and kicked a few leaves around to cover the traps and chains, and in the hope that the area would look undisturbed. We caught quite a few mountain beavers, which we killed and left in the woods and quite a few weasels and skunks, which we killed and skinned along with very few minks and a few muskrats. The weasel and skunk furs after we stretched and dried them sold in Shelton for about fifty cents each. The muskrat furs sold for about $3.00 apiece, and the minks for about $10 apiece. Mom wasn't pleased with our mishaps in occasionally pulling a trap out of hole that was clamped to the hind leg of a skunk.

We also looked for small animal trails near the creek and hid traps under leaves along these. We caught mainly muskrats and raccoons by the creek. The raccoon furs in good shape sold for about $1. Crawdads from the creek are one of their main food groups and they also catch frogs and garter snakes and wash them in the creek after they kill them, but before they eat them.

One night Gene took a flashlight down along our creek side trapping area to see if he could spot eyes looking at him and decide on that basis where to set his traps. He saw lots of eyes in the trees. The raccoons stay there at night to be safe from the bears and coyotes. The next few nights, he came back with his 22 rifle and shot a few raccoons out of he trees. But he only got fifty cents each for these hides because, he was told, they were damaged by the bullet holes. Several years later he was in the US Air Force telling his buddies about his teenage adventures. He told them that one night he took his rifle and a flashlight into the swamp and shot a few coons out of the trees. An Alabama boy said "My gawd, man, I thought we treated them pretty badly back home." Coon is southern slang for Negro.

Our trapping days and Leonard's rabbit raising days lasted for several years. We all liked to pet the rabbits, but Leonard was mainly interested in his profits from the furs and meat sales. He also sold baby rabbits as pets.

In the trapping business, Gene did most of the work including the skinning and drying of pelts and kept most of the proceeds. During this period, the state poisoned Spencer Lake (the poison was a chemical which absorbs all the oxygen from the water) to kill the non-game fish so it could be planted with bass. We went on a picnic there at the time and admired all the mink and raccoons crowding the waters edge away from the populated areas to feed on the belly-up fish. After WW II, several people in Mason County started mink farms to help meet the demand for mink fur. This eventually reduced the demand and price for wild mink furs.

~ *Hunting Seasons* ~

From junior high school on, Leonard and Gene took a week's sick leave from school each fall in hunting season to go hunting with Dad and Ronnie Gosser. After Gene bought a 30-06 rifle with his oyster earnings, Dad insisted that I go along each weekend and use Gene's old 30-30 rifle.

I liked hiking in the woods in the summer, but I hated wandering through the woods in hip boots during continuous rainstorms in hunting season. Also, the idea of shooting a deer didn't appeal to me.

The general approach to deer hunting was to have one or two of us (usually Dad and /or Ronnie) stand on a stump at the edge of a thicket while the rest of us slowly wandered through to scare the deer out. In elk season, we all wandered through the woods trying to stir up an elk herd. Most hunting licenses were for buck deer and bull elk only. These were sold for the state at sports shops. I don't remember ever getting one. We took sack lunches and returned to the car to retrieve and eat them around noon each day. We left home about 7am when it was still dark and came home about 7pm in the dark.

The area around Camp Grisdale was where we elk hunted, but most of the deer hunting was closer to home. We quenched our thirst by drinking out of the streams we crossed. Ronnie once questioned whether this was safe, but Gene observed that frogs lived along the streams so the water must be okay.

On the way to Camp Grisdale there was a sharp U-turn in the road with an old rotten log in the middle. One morning Dad decided to create a little excitement for us. He engaged Ronnie in a long winded conversation and sped up to about 50 mph as he approached the U-turn with his old Dodge. But instead of rounding the curve, he veered off the road, smashed through the old rotten logs, cut back onto the road, and kept going without a break in his conversation.

One morning, we chased an old doe out past Dad who shot and killed it before he could see that it didn't have horns. Since our licenses were for bucks only, we left the doe and went back to the car for lunch. At lunch I said, "On yonder hill lies a poor old doe who couldn't get out of the way of a hunter's bullet." Dad said, "Will you shut up and forget about that?" I said, "I might shut up, but I'll never forget about it."

Another time Dad said to me "Why don't you shape up and try to be a hunter?" I said, "I'll never make a hunter." Dad said, "You might make one, but you'll never be one."

Once when we sat down by the car to eat our lunches, Leonard said, "It smells like shit around here." Dad said, "Shut up and eat your lunch." Leonard discovered that he had sat down next to where some previous hunter had defecated. He said, "It is shit. Some dirty bastard shit right here!" Dad said, "For God's sake shut up and let the rest of us eat our lunches!"

Dad had a friend who made his own moonshine whisky. On the way home from hunting one evening, he stopped to visit. His friend whipped out a jug, took a swig, and offered it to Dad who took a swig and passed it to Leonard who took a swig and passed it to Gene. Leonard nearly choked on it, and asked Dad "Why didn't you warn me to only take a small sip of this stuff." Dad said, "How could I warn you? It took me a few minutes to get my voice back!" Gene spilled a little on the floor and their host's young son dashed in with a rag and mopped it up. Gene asked, "Why did you bother?" The son said "Ma makes me do it so that stuff won't eat a hole in the floor".

One elk season, I managed to shoot an elk in the rear as it passed me. I chased it and shot it in the rear several more times. It was limping badly and oozing blood and guts from several holes when it started to cross a road. Several guys jumped out of a car and shot it a few more times. Meanwhile our party had killed two elk back where we first saw them. As I walked into the road, Dad was right behind me. One of the road hunters said, "You might have wounded her (it was cow as well as bull elk season), but we finished her off so she's our elk." Dad looked at all the bullet holes and discolored flesh and said, "Yep, she's your elk. Come on, Daymond."

Another time we shot at several elk that rushed out of sight looking very agile. We spread out about 20 feet apart and walked after them looking for blood. I picked up a stone with a drop of blood on it and showed it to Dad a little later. He asked me where I found it and I said, "Back there." He said "when you find blood, you're supposed to immediately call everyone over to try to find the rest of the wounded elk's trail!"

One day we parked on a ridge above the Satsop River and hiked down across the river to get to our planned hunting area. The river was in its early flood stages and Ronnie got washed off his feet into a deep hole with a large rock in the middle. He managed to scramble on to the rock, soaked to the skin, with his rifle. After several attempts to reach him, we dragged a fallen small tree to the river's edge and leaned it across to Ronnie. He sat with his teeth chattering and said the he wasn't up to getting back into the water with his rifle. So Gene pulled himself along the tree to the rock, got Ronnie's rifle, and Ronnie by the hand and pulled him back to shore. Ronnie took off his pants to wring them out. His kneecaps seemed to be vibrating about an inch back and forth as he put his pants back on.

Washington allowed year-around bird and predator (bear, coyote, cougar) hunting. This allowed anyone to be in the woods with a rifle or shotgun at any time except at night with a flashlight. Shooting at eyes that reflect a light at night was illegal. But game wardens were usually only out and about in hunting season.

About 1950, the game department was notified that there were very few pheasants in an area where they used to be hunted.

They did a survey and asked a chicken farmer in the area if he would have his chickens hatch pheasant eggs if they provided them and paid him for expenses plus a bonus. He agreed and received about four-dozen pheasant eggs one spring day which he placed in spare chicken coops and nested hens on them. Most of them hatched and a game warden checked on them about six months later. As the warden watched, he opened the coops and shooed the pheasants out. He was given a check for his efforts. He left the coops open until all the pheasants returned in the evening then he closed them and ate lots of pheasants through the winter.

The next spring the game warden was back with more eggs. Again the farmer collected his check and dined on pheasant.

The third spring, the game warden did not return. The farmer called and asked about more pheasant eggs. The game department told him that there still didn't seem to be any pheasants in the area, and that it may have been too brushy for them. Therefore they were ending the program. He begged with them and told them that he had seen lots of pheasants in the last two years. But they still dropped the program.

The deer and elk hunters all wore bright red hats so they wouldn't be mistaken for game by the other hunters. They also wore various colored rain clothes including hip boots for slogging through the wet brush and wading streams. A few of them were shot every year in spite of the red hats which may have been out of sight behind tree limbs or other obstacles at the time.

One freezing day a hunter placed a canvas tarp over his car to keep ice off the windshield. After half a day of wandering through the woods, he came over a ridge, saw something tan colored, blasted away at it, and destroyed his own car engine.

~ The Forest Festival ~

After World War II, the Shelton Chamber of Commerce decided that Shelton needed some celebration or parade to advertise our town and attract more tourists. This evolved into the idea of an annual summer weekend forest festival to advertise Shelton as a logging and wood products center. Simpson had built up the bay area from several sawmills to additional plywood and paperboard mills. Raynier, a separate company, used sawdust from the mills to manufacture paper. Several trainloads of logs from Camp Grisdale in Olympic National Forest and numerous logging truck loads were dumped in the bay daily. Watching the trains come through town was one of my junior high school recess activities.

The Simpson Logging Company became the major sponsor of the Forest festival. They provided several floats for the parade including one wavy-armed box-shaped contrivance gaily painted to resemble a clown and operated, the first year, by Leonard inside. They also hauled several second growth fir logs, about three feet in diameter by 60 feet long with limbs on the top several dozen feet, to the high school football field where they were planted upright in the ground. These were tackled by competitive teams. First, at the sound of the starting gun, men with a pole climbing belt and spurs with a chain saw attached to the belt would climb each tree and top it (saw off the top just below the limb line). The winner was the man whose tree top hit the ground first. Then two man teams with crosscut saws would saw down each pole. There was a winning speed team and a winning accuracy team. The accuracy goal was to have the top of the pole squarely hit a stake preset for that purpose and drive it into the ground. Then the teams would speed compete in sawing their logs into several shorter logs.

At the end of the spring term each year, the Shelton High senior class would elect a Forest Festival Queen, several princesses and a (large senior) Paul Bunyan. They would be featured in the parade and evening festivities at the football field. Paul Bunyan rode on the top log of a loaded logging truck in the parade. The queen and her princesses rode on a flower decorated float. There were other competitive floats. The school band marched and played. Simpson provided a painter to paint float decorations and a scenic backdrop for the evening festivities. Dad volunteered each year to wire the stage lights and other areas as needed and remove the lights and wiring afterwards.

The stage wiring occurred in parallel with practice by the queen, her court, Paul Bunyan, and the high school thespian society of an evening skit. A neighbor noted that during this activity Dad socialized with the young ladies. He asked Mom as Dad listened in, "Don't you worry about Lank getting fresh around all those lovely young ladies?" Mom replied with a serious look "No, he's too fine, too noble, too old".

The forest festival became a popular annual mid-June celebration which drew many out of town visitors. The

Chamber of Commerce next observed that a large number of Christmas trees were harvested annually in Mason County and passed through Shelton mostly on their way to be sold in California. Christmas tree farming was becoming popular. So they nicknamed Shelton Christmas Town, USA.

Simpson's had started seriously replanting Douglas Fir trees in each new logged over area. Some of these also started disappearing as each Christmas season neared. We had volunteer young fir trees at the edge of our field and Dad found that it was well worth his time to provide a few of these to the annual harvest.

~ Bears and a Raccoon! ~

One spring day when Gene was out for a nature hike in Deer Creek Swamp, he noticed a large hole about 15 feet above the ground in a decaying fir snag (dead tree). There was a smaller partially uprooted tree leaning against the snag about five feet below the hole. Gene walked up on the leaning tree and looked in the hole. He was nose-to-nose with a hibernating bear. The bear started moving its head out of the hole and Gene jumped backwards off the tree. He ran home, got his rifle and a flashlight, came back and threw pieces of wood at the hole from the ground until the bear poked its head out again. He shot and killed the bear as it was halfway out of its den. Then he approached carefully up the leaning tree, made sure the bear was dead, and pulled the body out of the hole. After it dropped to the ground he shone the flashlight around inside the den to see what it looked like. It looked like two little orphaned bears staring back at him.

After he realized that he had killed their mother, Gene reached in and got a cub by the scruff of its neck in each hand. They only weighed a few pounds apiece. Gene carried them and his rifle home for Mom to admire. She got two old baby bottles, filled them with milk, snuggled the bears down on her lap in a big chair and fed both of them.

With tender loving care, the bears grew rapidly. They explored the yard, were cuddled by all of us, and learned to climb the smaller trees behind where our outhouse used to be.

It was torn down after we got piping from our canal and indoor plumbing.

The canal was split above the pump house and ditched across our field to behind the barn where the winter flow provided a large puddle. That winter, the bears liked to play in this puddle and got muddier than we ever did.

By their first June, the bears were in perpetual motion. Dad had Gene hold one in each arm to get some pictures for the Forest Festival. But they wouldn't face the camera. So Dad handed it to Mom and stood directly behind Gene and grabbed each bear from behind by the scruff of the neck. He held their heads towards the camera and turned until Mom told him she couldn't see him and took several pictures. In the pictures, Gene appeared to have four legs.

One sunny day Mom washed the bed sheets and hung them over the clothesline to dry. The line was about seven feet high and the sheets hung to near the ground. The bears found that these made fine swings. They instantly became unpopular with Mom who attacked them with a broom and chased them up the nearest tree to loud cries of wah, wah, wah! She took the sheets back inside and hung them in our upstairs bedroom to dry. During the summer they got into many other things and frequently got chased up the nearest tree with Mom and her broom in hot pursuit.

After about a year the bears were big enough to seriously

damage things and their meat consumption (mostly venison) was becoming painful. Dad offered them to the Seattle Zoo, but they stated that they already had plenty of black bears. Dad was friendly with a former Navy serviceman, Bud Mitchum, whom we met through our cousin, Chuck Cocherl. He ran a service station in Oregon City, near Portland. He offered to take the bears and built an 8x8x8 foot cage for them by his station using screwed together pieces of steel water pipes. He hung an old tire swing in the cage for them and often put on boxing gloves and got in and boxed with them. He hung a sign on their cage "see the genuine Oregon bears." They were a good attraction but after about six months, they started ganging up on him in the boxing bouts and he decided that their food bill was getting pretty high so he offered them to the Portland Zoo. This zoo also had plenty of black bears (which are usually brown) but they accepted the two as being unusually healthy looking and playful.

The winter after Gene brought the bear cubs home was when we started trapping and when Gene shot a few raccoons out of the maple trees along Cranberry Creek. One of the raccoons had a baby, which he brought home and kept in an old chicken coop. It was also a hit with everyone. We loved to give it a cookie and watch it wash it away in its water dish as it prepared to eat it. It would then sit with a perplexed look staring into its water dish. Its main diet items were provided by Mom but supplemented by crawdads and frogs, which we caught in the creeks. It washed everything before eating it.

After a few months the raccoon was half grown and the novelty had worn off. Gene took it back to where he found it and turned it loose.

When Gene later told his Air Force buddies about his fur trapping and the bears and raccoon, they concluded that he was a good storyteller, but had probably made it all up.

Some relatives of Bud Mitchum, the Pervisses, moved to Shelton and tried to sponge off our parents. Dad reacted negatively to this and they did not become family friends.

~ Additions and Repairs ~

In 1947 Dad decided that we should have a fruit orchard
and a storage cellar (like Grandad's). We already had a very
productive crab apple tree grown from a discarded core and
many volunteer plum trees, which were spreading between
our house and the chicken house. These were not in our side
garden plot, which had raspberry vines, a volunteer never-
bearing grape, and a volunteer logan berry vine. This plot was
recently plowed and was adjacent to the driveway into our
garage. It did not get watered regularly.

Dad bought several small greenhouse apple trees (saplings),
and a walnut sapling and planted them in his new orchard
area. Gene immediately adopted one of the apple trees and I
adopted another. The trees grew rapidly for the first year, but
didn't have any fruit. The volunteer plum trees had lots of fruit,
but they grew in a dry, grassy area, never got watered, and
grew hard dried up plums, which were mostly ignored, even by
the birds.

During the spring rains, Gene dug up the area around his
apple tree and fertilized it. It had several apples that fall, but
this treatment did not get repeated. The trees grew up but
the orchard essentially failed from neglect. Many years later,
a well was drilled next to this orchard to replace the Daygene
Canal water (which was somewhat muddy in the winter). Then
the orchard occasionally got watered and had fruit regularly
except the walnut tree. It probably suffered from lack of

pollination because there were no other walnut trees within many miles. But it had several walnuts most years.

With the orchard planted, Dad recruited us boys and started digging a cellar under the opposite end of the house from the entry door (the front door since it faced the entry driveway). We hauled the dirt in a wheelbarrow and dumped it about a dozen feet away in the front yard. Dad planned to line our new cellar with concrete blocks when it was done. But, after a good start, the sides kept caving in threatening to undermine the house foundation, and it was abandoned. We had an elongated hole about three feet deep and six feet wide, and eight feet long and a bumpy, hilly front yard. The hole was used to store stuff that eventually got burned or hauled out and dumped in the woods.

Dad didn't like the looks of the hole under the house, so he built a front porch about six feet wide over it, and installed a front door and steps. He roofed it and put in a clothesline for rainy weather clothes drying. He put a railing around it and supplied it with an old overstuffed couch. The railing became our favorite perch for blowing bubbles.

We got reject Simpson products almost for free. One day, Dad brought home a carload of reject insulating tiles, and lined the upstairs ceiling, which consisted of the slanting inside of the roof. Since this was the boys' bedroom, he asked us what color we would like to have him paint it. Gene asked if it could be light blue with pink polka dots. So it was baby blue with three-inch diameter pink circles about eighteen inches apart.

After Dad installed indoor plumbing, he built a cesspool (covered hole in the ground) about 2x4x3 feet deep beside the garage driveway and installed a drain to it from the indoor bathroom.

The garage had a dirt floor and open area adjacent to where the car was parked. After Dad got Mom an electric clothes washer, he decided to add a partition between the car and the rest of the garage to form an enclosed utility room for the clothes washer and a drain to the outside. Then he decided to pour a concrete floor for the entire area. After he got enough cement, he made wooden forms and had us help him mix, pour, and level the concrete. We arranged it so that the drain in the floor for the washing machine was at a low spot. A hose and tap provided the water source with some stove-heated water from inside the house. Later Dad added a hot water heater and taps next to the washing machine and also over the kitchen sink.

Several years later, Dad noticed that the logs the house was originally mounted on were rotting away. He borrowed some heavy-duty industrial jacks. He got a supply of 6x6x12 inch concrete blocks then sequentially jacked up each side of the house, moved the remains of the logs, dug a level trench, and laid and cemented a three-block high row of concrete blocks on each side.

Shortly after replacing the base of the house, Dad started re-roofing. The old cedar shakes had grown a layer of moss and started leaking. One summer, he tore these off in sections, and replaced them with fireproof synthetic shingles. The new foundation and shingles were still there 50 years later.

The lower edge of the house roof is about 10 feet off the ground. One day as Dad was working away and the usual group of small neighborhood kids had gathered to watch, he fell off the edge of the roof and landed on his back. As he lay there groaning on the ground, the kids all started shouting, "Do it again!"

The next day, he brought a raw oyster out with him. Before he got on the roof, he swallowed it for his audience. They seemed impressed, and he told them that raw oysters were so good that he sometimes tied a string on one so he could pull it up and swallow it again a few times. He offered to help a volunteer try it, but he didn't get any takers.

A few years later, Dad got some white asbestos tile shingles and shingled the outside of the garage. In 1956 Neil was killed in a car accident and Mom became depressed. He asked Mom if she would like him to build anything. She asked for a green house like her dad had. So he built a concrete block base glass-covered wooden frame greenhouse between the house and garden, and she started raising flowers and selling potted hanging baskets of geraniums. She had previously joined a Shelton flower club and obtained extra income by picking sword fern fronds along Cranberry Creek. She bundled them up and sold them to a Shelton flower shop for greenery in flower arrangements. She picked sacks full of moss from the maple trees along the creek to use as lining for her hanging baskets. She developed a small business selling baskets full of blooms in the spring and summer for $3.00 each. Dad made the baskets for her out of scrap wood and pieces of tree limbs.

The greenhouse was Mom's main hobby until she was in her late eighties and unable to tend to it anymore. Dad and Mom both enjoyed playing pinochle and joined several weekly clubs. Dad also became a member of the Masonic Lodge and Mom joined the women's auxiliary.

The greenhouse

~ After High School ~

When the class of "49" graduated from high school, Gene got
a job in Camp Grisdale with the Simpson Logging company
working in the cookhouse, and the following year, setting
chokers. When a tree is sawed down and a log of a desired size
is cut, the choker setter pulls a slack cable which runs from
a donkey engine through a pulley at the top of a spar tree to
the end of the fallen log. He loops the cable around the end of
the log and hooks it like a noose. This is the choker. He then
gets safely out of the way, and the donkey engine cranks in the
cable dragging the log with it. Some chokers for smaller logs
are connected to large bulldozers which drag the logs out to a
logging truck or train loading area.

Camp Grisdale was a self-contained town with housing for
the employees and families and a large mess hall with cooks
to feed the loggers who were among the country's better fed
citizens. In his first year, Gene's main job was in the mess
hall, but he filled in for absentees as a choker setter. It was a
risky job because if the log jammed against something, and
the choker pulled loose or the cable snapped, the loose end of
the cable would snap back. If anyone wasn't clear of the area,
the snapped cable could cut them in two or, at least, severely
damage them.

Gene saved his earnings and bought a new Ford sedan. The old
model-A Ford was driven into the bushes back of our chicken
house and left to rust. His new car could easily go 90 mph

and he set new records for the time from Camp Grisdale to Shelton. But one Friday night, near a farm by the community of Matlock, a black cow was standing in the middle of the road. Gene hit her broadside at about 70 mph. He said the cow sprawled across his hood and her tongue licked his windshield, but she was dead. The farmer wanted Gene to pay for his cow, but Gene refused on the basis that she shouldn't have been in the road, and that the farmer should pay for damages to his Ford.

One Sunday night three loggers in a Model-A Ford were returning to camp when they ran over a black bear and stalled with it thumping and growling under the car. They sat in the car afraid to get out for several hours until it freed itself and left. Then they waited until daylight before they were brave enough to get out and crank the Ford to start it again.

The Simpson Logging Company was unhappy with the bears. They had developed a taste for the bark of young fir trees and were killing a lot of the newly planted trees by chewing the bark off. Simpsons offered a $2.00 bounty for bear ears. Gene started taking his 30-06 rifle to Camp Grisdale with him and hanging around the camp garbage dump in the evening. He killed about a dozen bears and was the main collector of the Simpson bounty.

After graduation, Dad got Leonard odd jobs at the mill in Shelton. He also saved enough to buy a newer car and the old Model-A Ford joined Gene's in the bushes behind the chicken house. They are both still there rusting away.

After the war, Simpsons developed their Mason Lake property as an employee recreation area. Dad's group had a Saturday summer picnic there each year. They had a softball game between two groups in the afternoon. In 1950, Dad recruited Gene and me as left and right outfielders. The first fly ball to right field went over my head. The bases were loaded and when I got it, I couldn't decide where to throw it. A pop fly became a home run by the time I tossed it back to the infield. Dad was clearly annoyed but didn't say anything to me.

When Mark E. Reed died, he left an endowment fund to pay for scholarships for Simpson employees' children. In my last year of high school, I applied for and was awarded a $600 per year Reed Scholarship to the University of Washington to major in electrical engineering. That was sufficient to pay most of my yearly college expenses.

In 1950 when I graduated from high school in June, Gene decided to take his two week vacation from Simpsons (Camp Grisdale) to go on a sightseeing vacation. He invited me to go with him. We drove in his new Ford across Washington, north through the SE corner of British Columbia to the Trans-Canadian Highway, east into Alberta, south through Glacier national Park, on through Yellowstone Park, west to Portland on Highway 30, back to Olympia on Highway 99, and home. We pulled off the road and slept in sleeping bags beside the car each night.

On the Alberta plains we frequently saw weasel size brown animals scurrying around. We decided they must be lemmings and tried to catch one several times. Once we saw one run into a culvert under the road. Gene stopped and had me stand on one end of the culvert to jump on it as he threw rocks in from the other end to scare it out. It came out at about 30 mph and vanished in the weeds before I had a chance to jump. We found a dead one that had been hit by a car and threw it onto the back floor mat of the Ford. When we stopped for dinner, which was usually a hamburger and a milkshake, we asked our waitress about them. She told us they were prairie dogs. The next day, we drove back across the border to Glacier Park. The Canadian customs agent asked Gene if we were bringing anything back from Canada. Gene said "Yes, a dead prairie dog." We threw it away shortly after that.

Glacier Park had beautiful mountain scenery and we saw a black bear, and stopped to take a few pictures (with Gene's camera).

In Yellowstone Park, we stopped to admire a bear sitting in the ditch. Gene grabbed his camera and rolled down the window. The bear ambled over to the open window and stuck his head in to look for food. Gene slid rapidly to my side of the car and we both jumped out just ahead of the bear's nose. When the bear left, we got back in and drove on with a picture of its head poked in the window. We stopped a little later where another car was stopped to take a picture of a bear cub. Gene approached with his camera from the other side and found himself between the cub and its mother. She charged up to him, reared up and put a paw on each shoulder, growled in his face, then dropped down again. He was too shocked to get a close-up picture.

We stopped to view the Old Faithful Geyser. Gene was thirsty so he got a drink from a nearby stream. He spit it out again. It was sulfur spring water. We took pictures of several very colorful mud spouts. I read somewhere that one winter several hundred years ago, a trapper fell through the ice on a nearby pond. With his supplies wet, he couldn't start a fire. So he jumped into one of the hot mud ponds to stay warm until his partner found him and started a fire and rinsed and dried his clothes.

We tried to stop at night by potable water to brush our teeth and get a drink before we turned in. One night we stopped by a weedy looking pond. As Gene started to get a drink, I told him that it looked pretty stagnant to me. He said, "Nonsense, it has a frog in it," and proceeded to get a drink.

After we got home, Gene found an ad for a one year diesel engine maintenance school in Portland. He talked Leonard into taking it with him and they left in the fall and rented an apartment together. The ad said that there was a great demand for qualified diesel engineers and high paying jobs for their graduates were guaranteed.

I was still 17 when I graduated from high school, but most full time jobs required you to be 18. So I spent another summer working on the oyster beds. After that, with the Speeces gone, Lawrence hired some other local teenagers. He complained that neither his boys nor the other local boys were willing to work as hard as we did.

~ The Slaters ~

The Slater parents were retired and lived in Shelton Valley where they had several cows and a vegetable garden. Hewitt Slater was in my high school class and had three older sisters and a younger sister, Ann. Mrs. Slater was peripherally involved in the 4-H and was favorably impressed by me. She encouraged Hewitt to associate with me and he invited me to visit at their place several times.

Hewitt also became friendly with Leonard and Gene. He started hunting with them on weekends. Once he tried to fool them into thinking they heard a buck stomping. They were nearby but out of sight. He started thumping the butt end of his rifle on an old log. He really got their attention when the rifle went off and shot off his hat.

Mrs. Slater arranged for me to get together with Ann during the summer after my college freshman year. Since we seemed to like each other she arranged for Hewitt and a date, Della Adams, and me and Ann to take a drive (Hewitt drove the Slater family car) to the Paradise Inn area on the north slope of Mt. Rainier for an afternoon hike.

It started out as a pretty quiet drive so I started rattling away. Among other things, I noted that a delta was a triangular deposit at the mouth of a river and that Della was almost an appropriate name for Hewitt's date because she had a somewhat triangular shaped bottom.

After we got parked at Paradise Inn, Hewitt and I started a four-mile hike up to a mountain climbing staging area at about 10,000 feet elevation. The mountain is 14,408 feet high. Paradise Inn is at the 5500-foot level and is snowed in from October till May. The girls seemed glad to see us disappear.

After a two-hour hike, Hewitt and I were at the staging area, which had a concrete blockhouse for leaving some supplies or sleeping overnight prior to an ascent to the summit and back. As we were sitting admiring the scenery, Ann appeared. She had trailed us from a distance. I had my camera and a passerby took several pictures of the three of us.

Mount Rainier is an extinct volcano whose last eruption about 1000 years ago blew off about 1500 feet of peak and left a large flat-topped area which is packed with ice. This created the most glaciers, 23, of any peak in the contiguous 48 states. In summer the mountain meadows bloom and look like giant flower gardens.

It took us two hours to hike back down the mountain. We met Della near the inn, basking in the summer sunshine and left for our two-hour drive home just before dark.

My drippy behavior towards the girls was partly from a fear that I would fall in love and get married and thus terminate my college career. I could not imagine being a married student even though several of my classmates were (mostly the military veterans studying on GI scholarships).

Later in the summer, Hewitt and another date took Ann and me to an area of cascading water falls in the Olympic Mountains called "The Staircase." It is also a lovely area and we had a picnic by a small lake and tested the water for swimming. It was pretty cold, but we all dove in and splashed around.

My prattle during the drive might have been somewhat more tasteful than before, but Ann was turned off. She had just graduated (a year behind me) from high school and, in a short while to her mother's dismay, married one of her high school boyfriends. Hewitt also got married about that time.

When I was in college, the Slater parents decided to retire again. They built a small cabin near Bayshore, four miles from Shelton and two miles from us on Big Shookum Bay. They bought a rowboat and set up a picnic area with a wood-burning grill. They got a rock tumbler (polisher) and collected, polished, and decorated the area with beach pebbles. They invited their children and friends to come use their facilities at any time but to call ahead of time.

After I was married and had kids, we had many afternoon picnics there and I rowed the kids back and forth across the bay (about one-quarter mile each way) and visited with the Slaters. So did Gene and his family. We also had many summer picnics at the Simpson Employee Recreation Area on Mason

Lake along with Mom, Leonard, and Doris and their families.

We had picnics several times at Slaters' area with Hewitt and his family and once when Ann and her family were there. Hewitt told me that she asked him several times why I was such a drip on our teenage outings.

~ My First Year of College ~

Mark E. Reed's will specified that starting in 1949 and within the Simpson Logging company working area, a single Mark E. Reed College Scholarship be awarded each year. I was very pleasantly surprised to be the 1950 winner. I was also the graduating class saludatorian. Each summer, the scholarship board hosted a banquet at the Colonial House in Shelton for the past and present winners. The Colonial House was once the home (mansion) of the Reed family. My first of these was the finest meal I had ever had.

In the fall, I enrolled in the University of Washington Electrical Engineering course (EE). I got accepted into a co-op house (rental home for students) near the University of Washington campus. It housed over a dozen students who elected officers and a house manager to manage it.

My first exposure to the electrical engineering (EE) curriculum was to take an entrance exam. To my surprise, I flunked trigonometry and had to take a beginners (remedial) course. I learned that most of the Seattle high school graduates had already studied calculus, which I had not previously heard of.

Most of the basic engineering courses, like blueprint drawing, were pass or flunk courses, and if you passed you got a "C." My first quarter, I was sure I was flunking out. By the end of the first year, I had achieved a "B" average, and a big dose of increased confidence.

In the '50's, the universities had metal Quonset huts for housing GI's who were on military funded university educational programs. All non-veteran male students were required to take two years of Reserve Officers Training Corps (ROTC). I chose Air Force (USAF) ROTC and did well in the classroom training, but poorly in marching exercises for which we wore uniforms.

In the first two years, gymnastic courses were required. In the first year, they included exercises, wrestling, boxing, and swimming. I hated boxing and did poorly at it.

For holidays, I called Mom and specified a time to meet me at the Seattle to Bremerton ferry run in Bremerton, 24 miles from home. Then I took a bus to the ferry landing and met them in Bremerton. I enjoyed the hour-long ferry rides. I like to stand by the back upper deck railing and watch the seagulls swoop for food scraps some people tossed them and watch the scenery go by. Some less charitable souls tossed the seagulls lighted cigarette butts.

Sherwood house had a ping pong table and after a while, I thought I was a pretty good player. A Chinese student tried to teach me to play chess, but on the first trial game, he beat himself, became irritated, and terminated the lessons.

In the spring of 1951, we had a pre-finals Friday night beer party. The white poodle from next door wandered in. One of the seniors gave it a saucer of beer, dyed its tail pink, and sent it home. I thought we might hear about that later, but we didn't.

During my first year of college I faithfully attended the local Methodist church and joined a college youth group. By the end of the year, I was very skeptical of religion. I purchased a book on the world religions and was surprised to learn that the Old Testament is the Jewish Bible and that both the old and the new testaments and the Koran are the Muslim Bibles. Also, a multitude is said to have watched Mohammed ascend bodily into heaven. The first recorded source of the "golden rule" was Confucius.

I was somewhat mentored by one of the GIs at Sherwood House. He sold me a captured German field camera with a slide-in frosted plate in back showing the picture to be taken. He also talked me into buying and wearing a hat. My next trip home, I carried the hat into the house and left it on top of my luggage. Mom picked it up later and asked, "Where did this man's hat come from?"

Most of my pictures were black and white but I took an underexposed colored picture of our Christmas tree. When it was developed, only the lit up light bulbs showed. I took my ROTC uniform home for Christmas vacation and had Lula take several pictures of me in uniform.

During my first year of college, the Washington Game

Department decided that the fish ladders of abandoned dams on local streams provided a salmon trap where the migrating salmon were easily gaffed by local boys. They dynamited many old dams including Castles dam on Cranberry Creek.

~ My Second Year of College ~

I got a job for the summer helping load box cars at the Simpson paperboard plant. The other three loaders invited me to play poker with them at lunch time, so I learned to play nickel ante poker and be bluffed out of winning hands. Several times, I volunteered to work a second shift for someone who didn't show up, usually at the plywood gluing machine. Plywood is made by shaving thin sections of wood off a rotating log somewhat over eight feet long. As the sheet of wood is shaved off, it is cut into sections about 4.2 feet long which are glued together in the gluing machine to reach the desired thickness and are then trimmed to four by eight foot sheets. The final step by the gluing machine is to press the sheets together and heat them until the glue dries which is only about a minute. The standard thicknesses are in eighth-inch increments up to three-fourths inch thick. I had sold my first car and rode to work and back with Dad.

Leonard and Gene finished up diesel school and couldn't find any diesel engineering jobs. The Korean War was in full force and the draft board was breathing down our necks. Leonard went to work for the Mason County Fire Department and got married. The draft board favored single people and he did not get called. Gene, Buddy Knutsen, and some high school friends volunteered for a four year hitch in the Air Force to avoid the Army. Part of the recruiting pitch which really appealed to Gene was that you could become a fighter pilot. Instead, after basic training, they told him he weighted too much and his blood pressure was too high. They assigned him to a ground crew, and sent him to an airbase in Korea during his second year.

I was awarded the $600 Reed Scholarship for a second year and went back to the University feeling somewhat wealthy. My roommate arrived on a hot afternoon after a 150 mile drive from Southern Washington with a case (12 bottles) of home brew (beer) he had brewed in a bathtub. After he hauled it into our room, we opened one to test it. It wasn't much of a sample because after the initial burst hit the ceiling and it quit foaming over, there was only a half-inch of warm brew in the bottom. He put the rest in our clothes closet and told me it would be calmed down by morning. We were both awakened in the middle of the night by some kind of explosion. He turned on the light, dashed to the closet, and discovered that two adjacent bottles had blown off their caps and soaked all our clothes with warm beer. He was afraid to touch his case again, so I carried it out to the fire escape (which was by our room) and left it there for the night. He was afraid to get near it, so I drank the rest of the beer over the following week.

Two of our housemates didn't return that fall. A buddy of theirs said that after finals, they decided to drive down Highway 99 from Seattle to Tacoma and stop and each have a beer at each bar along the way (about 50). He figured they probably died happy somewhere near the outskirts of Tacoma.

I felt more confident of my scholastic abilities in my second year. I did particularly well in math (an overreaction to having to take remedial trigonometry) and was picked for the college math honor society, Sigma Xi.

For gymnastics, we got to select second year courses. I signed up for sailing in the fall. The University (UW) had its own harbor on Lake Washington and a fleet of small sailboats.

In the winter, I took skiing. The University of Washington had it is own ski lodge and rental equipment on a Cascade mountain pass. I had a female instructor who told me that I was the most awkward thing she had ever seen on skis and that if I didn't break a leg, she would give me a "B." It was the only gymnastics class in which I didn't get a "C".

Near the end of the winter quarter, I packed snow under my wristwatch from numerous falls and got a frostbitten wrist. So I put my high school graduation wrist watch on my right hand. Later as several of our house members were playing softball in the street, I discovered that each time I threw the ball, my watch would follow it and land in the street. After a few throws, it was done for.

In the spring, I took golf. The university had its own 9-hole course and rental irons. I don't think I ever made par on a hole. Par is the number of hits an overage golfer is expected to take on each hole. I never played golf or went skiing again. When I was working for General Electric in Santa Barbara, California in 1960, however, I rented a small sailboat and took a date for an afternoon sail.

During the spring break, I visited with several of my college friends in southern Washington. I wrote Gene that I went bear hunting with them. Gene wrote back and said, "Hah! If you guys saw a bear you'd probably offer it a beer".

In December, 1951, Gene was home on leave for Christmas. There was snow on the ground and he had me take several pictures of him sprawled out on his back, in his uniform, eyes closed, with his rifle beside him. We had Lula take a picture of us with Gene hanging from a maple limb about 15 feet off the ground and me hanging on to one of his legs. I was supposed to be kicking wildly, but Lula had trouble determining how to use the camera and by the time she snapped the picture, I was pretty limp.

The following summer, the Shelton Methodist Church invited its college student members to address the members on Sunday. I talked about the various world religions, but I felt like I was criticizing my elders and I couldn't get my volume up to where anyone more than twenty feet away could hear me. But several front row people told me later that it was an interesting speech.

Gene was home again for two weeks leave during the summer. He had his Ford with him and parked it in the barn when he left to go to Korea. Dad told him that I was getting pretty husky and egged him into having a wrestling match with me. I promptly showed him all the wrestling holds I had learned in gym class. He was duly impressed and we called it a draw.

On Memorial Day, the ROTC had a parade on campus. It was a hot day and we were standing at attention afterwards for a speech by an Air Force officer. After about five minutes several of us, including me, passed out and fell down.

~ My Third Year of College ~

Lula graduated from high school in June 1952. She got accepted to the University of Washington for a major in journalism and got a summer typing job in town to save money.

I invited an Indian foreign exchange student to spend the summer with us. He was enrolled in a Ph.D program in chemistry and had obtained a summer job at the Simpson paperboard plant. Dad's long time boss at Simpsons hired me for the summer for an office job, typing up musty files of old maintenance reports and filing them by equipment types for quick accessibility and readability. He could have hired a female secretary, but it was a short term job, he wanted to help me along and the shop talk in the area got pretty raunchy at times. We both rode to work and back with Dad.

We hitch-hiked back to the university in the fall while Dad and Mom were getting Lula moved into a women's co-op house. The folks helped pay Lula's way. I felt rather rich with my summer wages and third Reed scholarship. But I wanted to buy a car. A friend helped me get hired by a neon sign rental company to check three nights a week on signs at several dozen locations around Seattle. The company provided a pickup truck for the job.

With an additional source of income I bought a 1942 Ford four-door sedan for $600. these were the last domestic cars

Ford produced before re-tooling for WW11 military vehicle production. Then I started exploring Seattle and Lula and I had our own transportation home during college breaks.

In the third year of electrical engineering, the students chose between power systems and electronics. I chose power systems so that after I graduated, I could work for the Bonneville Power Administration which controlled power distribution from the Columbia River dams and thus remain in Washington state.

For the fall term to my great surprise, I was elected house president. I finally began to realize that the Sherwood House crew regarded me as an equal rather than some inferior sissy. At our first weekly meeting, I made a motion that we not permit smoking during house meetings. This was boo'ed down without a vote. Later in the year, a buddy talked me into helping him practice blowing smoke rings using his cigarettes. In a week, I was hooked and buying my own cigarettes.

I was a two-pack-day smoker for the next forty years until I finally quit during chemotherapy after a colon cancer operation. The chemo poisons caused the cigarettes to have an unusually nasty taste. I also lost 30 pounds. I highly recommend chemotherapy to those who want to lose weight or quit smoking.

The word spread around Sherwood House that I had never had sex. One of the guys gave me the address and phone number of a nympho he had met at a party. I called her and visited her at her apartment. Over a cup of coffee, she told me a sad story of how she had been sexually abused by her dad and never had a happy relationship with a man. I felt sorry for her and started sympathizing. Then she told me that I should leave because her boss was dropping in. It was several more years before I had sex for the first time, with a prostitute for $20.

In the late winter as I was checking downtown Seattle neon signs, I was looking back as I approached a stop light and rear-ended a stopped car. I exchanged insurance data with the driver who claimed that his girl friend was pregnant and damaged by the light collision. The sign company insurance paid off some reduced amount from his threatened claim and I was fired.

Over my years at the university, I saw several familiar faces from high school. As I was walking by a sorority house on my way back from class, a young lady on the veranda said "Hi!" It was Karen Condon who was a year behind me in high school. We talked for a few minutes as several of her house mates listened in. As it ended, I said, "so long for now, Casey (her high school nickname after her initials: KC). Her housemates all echoed "Casey?" She never spoke to me again.

Panty raids were a new fraternity diversion in 1953. In one raid, the boys broke a sorority freshman's arm as she tried to defend the panties she was wearing.

One of the fraternities had a Saint Bernard dog as a mascot. They had trained it to stand crosswise on the sidewalk on cue. They amused themselves by having the dog block passing groups of coeds. If they tried to detour around it, it moved to block them again.

Another fraternity house had two red Irish setters as mascots. They were enrolled under phoney names in an American literature program. The fraternity members took turns attending classes answering roll call and taking exams for their mascots. After four years, both Irish setters were to be graduated with honors until some curmudgeon revealed the scheme.

Sherwood House used the member fees to hire a cook and buy provisions for regular meals. In addition, there was a pot for donations for Friday beer busts. In the spring, money started disappearing from this pot. Several keepers of the pot started watching it at night through the keyholes in their doors. They caught an Indian foreign exchange student robbing it. He was confronted and expelled from the house. He was not doing well in engineering school, and later committed suicide by leaping off the nearby Lake Washington canal bridge. The canal adjacent to the university was for ship traffic between Lake Washington and Elliott Bay.

There was a large yacht marina on Union Bay midway between

Lake Washington and Elliott Bay. Most of the yachts had very high masts so that the canal drawbridges had to be raised every time they sailed through.

One holiday Saturday, I drove one of my friends to Mount Rainier, which is visible 100 miles away from the UW campus on a clear day. We hiked up the mountain and back. On the way back on a long straight stretch, I sped up to about 90 miles per hour to see how my car handled at high speed. A highway patrolman stopped me and gave me a speeding ticket. This was my first run-in with the law and it gave me a nearly uncontrollable case of the shakes while he was writing the ticket.

On another school break, Sherwood House had a picnic in the park. I told several friends that I thought I could hold a newly opened beer above my mouth and drink the beer as fast as it ran out. They questioned whether that was possible, so I gave a demonstration. They called their friends and asked me to do it again. I did, but that night my mouth and throat were white and felt raw.

On one trip home, I decided to teach Lula how to drive. On a long empty straight stretch, I got her to pull out in low gear and shift the gears to second and high as she sped up. We were coming from the Bremerton ferry landing and traffic was light. For the next ten miles she drove about fifty miles per hour and was feeling pretty confident as we approached the turn off to Moms at Cranberry Creek Road. I told her to slow down, but she didn't hit the brakes until just before our right turn. We sailed into the bushes and into a barbed wire fence and finally stopped. I backed the car out and drove the final quarter mile home. Lula refused to try to drive again until years later after she was married, moved to California, and needed transportation to a new job with the California Welfare Agency. Her husband was from California and met her in Shelton after he got out of the navy in Bremerton.

In the spring, the university arranged job interviews for both summer jobs and post graduation jobs. I interviewed for and accepted a summer job with General Electric at the Hanford Plutonium manufacturing plant on the Columbia River in central Washington.

Sherwood House had a paid student housekeeper to buy supplies for our meal cook, arrange for repairs when needed, manage our bank account, pay the cook, collect and deposit room payments, and other miscellaneous things. I applied for and got this job for my senior year.

~ The Summer of 1953 ~

After finals, Lula and I loaded up the Ford with our goodies and I drove us home. After a few days relaxation, I loaded my stuff up again and drove to Richmond, Washington. I rented a room for the summer in a single men's dormitory and moved in.

For many years, General Electric managed the Hanford facilities for the US government as the US production facility of plutonium, the primary ingredient of hydrogen bombs. The facility covers hundreds of square miles of desert along the Columbia River north of the town of Richmond. There are half a dozen production plants miles apart. They are accessed by paved highways from Richmond and between them. The entire area is surrounded by a wire mesh fence with a guard station at the highway entrance. The workers are transported to and from Richmond by bus. There was a fleet of Buicks with governors to limit their top speed to 50 mph. These were used for transporting managers and materials between plants.

For much of the summer, I drove one of the Buicks as a chauffeur and delivery boy. I also did low-level engineering analysis for my assigned supervisor and attended informational briefings aimed at encouraging the summer employees to join General Electric after they graduated.

On weekends between beer parties with the dorm residents, I explored the local area both by car and on foot. Several times, I chased jack rabbits down hills. I avoided the bushy areas along the river which we were told posed a danger from rattlesnakes.

I drove home to celebrate my birthday on the Fourth of July weekend. After I got back, several friends treated me to a beer party the following Saturday night. We finally stumbled off to bed about 3:00am. When I finally got up Sunday, the dorm was all smoked up and the couch I had been sitting on was outside badly burned. That was the only time I ever ignited a cigarette fire.

On Saturday, I drove up Mount Adams with a friend and explored the environment above the timber line. We saw a bear in the distance. As we were leaving, we got into a discussion of how fast a man could run if pursued by a bear. I said that on a downhill slope, I could run at least 15 mph for a short distance. He was very skeptical so I had him drive on the next stretch and clock me. I averaged 16 mph for the several hundred yard stretch. But I told him that bears can hit 25 mph on level ground.

A story made the rounds that on a routine radiation check, one of the buses was definitely radioactive. Using geiger counters, the security office found radioactivity at one of the bus stops in Richmond and tracked it to a worker's home. He was very radioactive and confessed to putting one of the plutonium bricks in his lunchbox and taking it home as a souvenir of his job. The neighbor's wife, but not his own wife, was also radioactive. Both of them were stripped of radioactive clothing, which was burned, had their heads shaved, and were given a chemical bath. This same procedure was used at work when accidental radioactive exposures occurred.

The Hanford plant was built before the dangers of radioactive exposure were fully appreciated. The plants released enough radioactivity into the air that there was significant contamination of downwind sheep pastures and of the sheep. Cooling water seeped into the Columbia River and caused measurable radioactivity of the river water. Major filtering and containment efforts were subsequently implemented, but no money was awarded to those accidentally exposed to the earlier radiation.

On the Friday night after my final week at Hanford, I loaded up the Ford and drove home (about 200 miles). I was drowsy coming down from White Pass to Highway 99, and was thankful to get on a level highway. As I settled down to 60 mph, I heard gravel splattering and woke up to see the highway off to my left. I jerked the steering wheel that way. The front tire was still on the pavement and the car did one and a half spins and stopped while coasting backwards, the trunk flew open and my toolbox flew out, sprang open, and scattered tools around. Fortunately, there were no other cars either way and I had time to gather up my stuff, turn around, and drive on a few miles to the nearest coffee shop. After several cups of coffee and a half pack of cigarettes, I drove on home.

During my two weeks at home, Doris introduced me to one

of her high school friends and we dated for a while. This consisted mostly of movies in town and afternoon drives. On a drive to the Gosser oyster house to let her collect a few oyster shells, I let her drive up the mostly one way dirt drive along Deer Creek to the bay. One of the local men was speeding around a corner and crashed into us. Both cars were still operable and he left without introducing himself. Dad asked a few residents and found out who he was. Dad tried to get him to pay for the damage to my car, but finally gave up. I pulled out the dented front fender until it looked reasonably good. Lula and I rode it back to UW for the fall term a few days later.

~ *My Fourth Year of College* ~

When I got back to Sherwood house, the summer residents
pointed out my first housekeeper duty. The main sewer from
the house was plugged and the basement was a foot deep in
brown water full of toilet paper and floating turds. I called a
plumber who took a look and told me "I won't touch it until
you get that water out of here!" I took our lawn watering hose
and ran it out of the basement window. I had another house
member hold the outside end in the air as I connected it to
the basement sink faucet and filled it with water. Then I had
him plug the end with his thumb and pull it partway down
the hill behind the house. I unhooked it from the faucet and
submerged my end in the sewage water. As I held my end
down, I had him release his end and fling the hose down the
hill. This siphon then started draining the basement.

It took over an hour for the basement to drain as I kept the
hose pushed down to the bottom. I was wading in the goop
in an old pair of shoes with no stockings. When it finished
draining down the hill, I retrieved the hose and put it in the
sink. I called the plumber who came back and cleaned the clot
out of the sewer line. Then I hooked the hose up again and
flushed the basement residue down the drain. I washed and
put away the hose and my shoes. Then I looked down the hill.
In a corner of our neighbor's lawn was a four foot diameter
three- inch deep pile of sludge consisting mostly of soft turds
and toilet paper. I wondered afterwards how they reacted to it
and where they thought it came from. They must have noticed

it the next time they mowed their lawn.

I quickly got used to the housekeeping routine. One chore was the monthly cycling of two wall pictures from a local museum. One that I remember was of a wild-looking rearing satyr.

For part of the fall term, I was humor editor for the weekly engineering students' newsletter. By faculty request, I lost this job for publishing too many dirty jokes. One source of these was the newsletters from other UW student groups.

Separate AC and DC electric motor labs were required by the electrical power curriculum. Old motors were donated by the local industries and, in pairs, we had to plug them in, run them at various speeds, and write reports comparing measured performance to theory. An electronics lab and a magnetism lab were also required. In the DC motor lab, we were warned to be sure to plug in the motor field coil correctly or it would short circuit and might start a fire. My partner and I managed to prove that this was true.

In 1954, the UW engineering school responded to persistent complaints that old exams in the fraternity files gave the members an unfair advantage in studying for exams. So the files of old exams were opened to all the students. For some reason, the magnetics course and lab were hard for me to understand. The only exam was the final and I studied hard for it. But I did not review the previous final exam because that seemed like cheating. After that final, I feared that I had flunked the course, particularly after another student told me that the exam was identical to the previous year's final, which was studied by most of the class. But I got a "C".

We had a fluid dynamics class where I did well. But one of the fraternity boys sat next to me and copied my answers on the tests. He wanted to have me study the fraternity copy of the old final with him to prepare for the final exam. Although I refused, he showed it to me. Unlike the school files, his copy had the correct solution to each problem worked out. He memorized these before the exam.

For the exam, the instructor asked me to move away from the fraternity boy, which I did. The exams were passed out and they were identical to the previous one from the fraternity files, including the numerical values. I was so annoyed that I couldn't concentrate. The frat boy got the top exam grade in the class. The instructor contacted me later and asked what happened, but I didn't tell him.

One part of the fluid mechanics course was the study of the laminar airflow and the relationships between temperature, pressure, and velocity. Since pressure drops as velocity increases, airplane wings are shaped so that the air is forced to move faster over the topside than the bottom side. In a sense the reduced pressure on the top of the wing results in the airplane being pulled into the sky as it picks up speed for take-off.

A German scientist, Von Karmen, was a pioneer in the study of non-laminar airflow. When the original Tacoma Narrows suspension bridge over Puget Sound blew down in the 1930s, the immediate plan was to replace it with an identical bridge. Von Kamen warned that the new bridge would then blow down for the same reasons as the original. He presented an analysis and some recommendations for changes to modify the airflow in the high winds that were common in the Tacoma Narrows area. These modifications were included in the new design as well as in the design of the Golden Gate Bridge over the inlet to San Francisco Bay, and to later suspension bridges. After WWll, the wind tunnels designed for aircraft analysis were also used to refine suspension bridge designs and for wind stability analysis.

I bought a used portable typewriter after my first year of college and used it to type my reports. After I graduated, I gave it to my sister Doris.

My electric motors professor got me admitted to the engineering honor society, Tau Beta Pi, and encouraged me to apply for a once a year $2,000 Westinghouse scholarship for a masters program at Illinois Institute of Technology in Chicago. To my surprise and my draft board's irritation, I won it and obtained a scholastic draft determent for another two years. Westinghouse also provided me with my 1954 summer job at their electric power equipment manufacturing plant in East

Pittsburgh, Pennsylvania.

~ *My 1954 Summer Job* ~

Before the June 1954 graduation ceremonies, I arranged with
another graduating Sherwood House member who had
accepted an east coast job to meet me at home a week after
graduation and take me to East Pittsburg in exchange for me
paying for gas. I drove my dented-up Ford home and sold it to
my younger brother, Neil, per prior agreement.

My friend appeared on schedule and I loaded my stuff in his
car and said my goodbyes. We had a a pleasant four-day drive
to East Pittsburgh, which is a slum adjacent to the fenced
Westinghouse plant. It had several smelly flophouses hotels
and he dropped me off at one. The proprietor was surprised
to see a clean looking lad, but rented me a room for $10 in
advance. I moved my stuff in, blocked the door with a dresser
(it was also bolted), skipped dinner, and had a reasonably good
nights sleep.

In the morning, I carried my stuff to the gate guard who
looked at my job acceptance and map and pointed out where
to go for my new-employee orientation meeting. After the
meeting one of the personnel gave me a local area map
and showed me the location of the dorm where I had been
expected to spend the night. I had somehow missed that in my
instructions. He drove me there to drop off my stuff then back
and introduced me to my summer boss.

My summer assignment was to develop a general formula

for the performance of permanent magnets using extensive test data accumulated by Westinghouse. I tried multiple combinations of the magnet dimensions spacings, magnetic strength, and other characteristics, but could not arrive at a satisfactory performance formula. So I flunked my summer assignment and reported to Illinois Tech in the fall.

Initially, I got to work and back on the Pittsburg electric trolley system. After several pay checks, I bought a 1950 Studebaker sedan and started exploring the area. I joined an ad-hoc youth group. On a wild-lands hike, the trees all had a very dirty smudgy layer up to the highest six to ten feet. A fellow hiker told me that that marked the new growth in the few years since the steel mills were all required to implement ionic smoke precipitators on the smoke stacks.

Downtown Pittsburgh is at the intersection of the Allegheny and the Monongahela Rivers which is the start of the Ohio River. The Westinghouse plant is upstream on the Monongahela River which flows from the West Virginia mountains. It had bad winter floods. In the late forties, Westinghouse built a dam across the valley below their East Pittsburgh plant with a pump to pump the local creek over it during flood times. The downstream steel mills sued to prevent Westinghouse from closing the dam gates since this would restrict the natural flow plane of the river and increase their flood level (very slightly). Westinghouse regarded this as a frivolous lawsuit and ignored it. A local judge listened to the steel company arguments and issued an injunction forbidding

Westinghouse from using their dam.

The Allegheny River flows from north central Pennsylvania. One day, our group had a picnic on an Allegheny sandbar. I started to swim in the river, but was quickly discouraged by soft brown lumps (raw sewage) floating by.

On my way to Illinois Tech (Chicago) in the fall, I stopped in Marion, Ohio to visit for the first time with most of my uncles and aunts.

~ Illinois Tech ~

Illinois Tech is located on South State Street in Chicago where a Negro slum and a White slum meet. A slaughterhouse was about five miles southeast. When the wind blew from that direction, it would gag a goat. The biggest police force on the south side was the campus police. Chicago University had a ten-foot brick walled campus about ten miles farther south. Lake Michigan was a few miles east.

The campus dorms had automatic locking doors and each resident had his own key. Next to my room was an ancient six-story hotel being used as a Negro house of prostitution. Each Friday evening, a well-fed, well-dressed Negro in a Cadillac would stop there and collect his fees. One winter night, the place caught fire which was put out by a truck and ladder crew. The next day during a city damage assessment, it was found that for years, the building garbage had been dumped in the empty elevator shaft which had filled to the third floor. After an adequate payoff, the building was back in business as usual.

One night I was stopped near campus by an unmarked patrol car with two officers for speeding. One walked up to my Studebaker window and asked if I was a student. He told me they could let me go without a ticket if I showed his buddy some appreciation. I walked back to the patrol car, and said, "Gee, thanks", and got back in my car and left as they stared dumbfounded at each other.

There were several ten-story brick government low-income housing buildings just north of campus. The windows folded out for fresh air. In the summer, teenagers would carry bricks to the roof and see how many open windows they could break by dropping them off.

There was a crime wave in a well-to-do northern neighborhood. When residents were on vacation, they asked the police to watch their residences. One family also hired a private detective agency that arrested a group of Chicago policemen looting their house.

One night I took a bus to see a downtown movie. The return bus dropped me off near midnight a block from campus. It was winter and I was wearing an overcoat. Halfway across the block three teenage dopies jumped me and dragged me into an alley. I grabbed a drainpipe as two of them jerking my legs were bouncing me up and down on my back in a mud puddle while the third tried to reach under my overcoat to my wallet (which only had $10 in it). They heard someone coming, an old wino, and fled down the alley.

I hated Chicago in the winter. It was much colder than I was used to and the frequent snow falls blew up and down the streets and turned gray within hours of falling.

In addition to my graduate studies, I had undergraduate student teaching duties for an old bald German professor. One class was a DC motor test lab. Two students asked my help in hooking up their motor. As at UW, I managed to plug it in wrong and started a little fire. Another student grabbed the fire extinguisher and put it out.

I liked my other professors but the old German professor irritated me. He reminded me of an Al Capp cartoon character called "Bald Iggle." On final exam day, he asked me to watch the class like a hawk because several members were cheaters. I passed out the tests then drew a cartoon of his head on the board and wrote under it "Bald Iggle is vatchink you." Several students asked me to erase it before he wandered by and saw it. So I did.

I learned some new math at Illinois Tech including the theory and use of Laplace Transforms. I learned methods of analysis of short circuits on high voltage transmission lines and wrote my thesis on these. What I remember best of my graduate learning is that every year in the USA about 400 people (mostly fishermen and golfers), and 20,000 cows are killed by lightning, and that it is much more likely to strike repeatedly in the same place than elsewhere in the vicinity. In thunderstorms, cows tend to rush to the nearest tree and stand facing it. If lightening strikes the tree, the voltage gradient between their front and hind feet electrocutes them.

One of my friends at Illinois Tech was an Alabama red neck. I imitated his talking style until I picked up a southern accent. Women at parties sometimes asked me what part of the south

I was from. I usually replied "South Seattle, Ma'am".

Another friend had me follow him home to South Chicago one semester break and took me to a house of prostitution where I had my first sexual intercourse.

My draft board tried to reclassify me 1A (available) when I arrived at Illinois Tech, but Dr. Lewis (the dean of electrical engineering) wrote them a letter justifying a continued student deferment.

Near graduation, I applied for one of the 600 annual Science Foundation grants for an advanced degree. Having won the one-per year Mark E. Reed and Westinghouse scholarships, I thought I'd be a shoe-in, but I never heard back from them. I was shocked.

I worked another summer at Westinghouse and graduated after two years. I did well on most of my oral exam questions, but the math professor asked detailed questions that I could not answer on the theory of Laplace Transforms. I was awarded my MSEE (Master of Science Electrical Engineering) degree, but my thesis professor, Dr. Lewis, who was head of the department told me that I should work for a few years and mature more before pursuing any more advanced degrees.

Between Illinois Tech and East Pittsburg, I stopped several times to visit my Marion, Ohio relatives. One summer day, two of my uncles provided me with a shotgun and took me rabbit and pheasant hunting. My reactions were too slow to get a good shot whenever we flushed either one. I blasted both barrels at a pheasant we scared up. I missed the pheasant, but a cow standing in that direction started jumping. My uncles decided that was enough shooting for the afternoon. One cousin, Bessie May Cocherl, set me up with a girl friend. I came back at Christmas break and took her for a drive in my Studebaker with a broken heater. That cooled that romance.

That summer, the Washington State Game Department decided that logs across state streams provided platforms for boys to gaff salmon. They ran bulldozers up many streams including Cranberry Creek pushing the logs aside and leveling the stream beds. The following winter floods washed all the salmon eggs out of the gravel stream beds and after four years, nearly eliminated future salmon runs in those streams. Deer Creek was spared because the bulldozer operator gave up at Deer Creek Swamp. But the resultant much faster winter flow in Cranberry Creek washed out the Highway 3 bridge forcing the Shelton-Allyn traffic to detour via the Mason Lake Road. Dad's commute to Shelton was increased form six miles to sixteen miles for several months until a temporary Cranberry Creek bridge was built. It was nearly summer before a new permanent bridge was built.

~ Beyond College ~

From my job offers when I left Illinois Tech, I accepted one from General Electric in Lynn, Massachusetts. I wanted to become familiar with the United States, and the east coast seemed like a good place to start. I learned that GE had a graduate level three-year internally taught series of courses designated as the advanced engineering program, also known as the A, B, and C courses. These were each nine months long with a one half-day class and about 40 hours of homework in addition to 36 hours of work per week. On the basis of my MSEE, I managed to skip the A Course and enroll in the B Course. As part of the series each enrollee had a new work assignment each six months.

Ironically, one of the B-course problems was to develop an infinite series general formula for the performance of permanent magnets. In one weekend (with class guidance), I managed to solve the problem that I had failed to make any progress on during my summer at Westinghouse.

For the C Course, there was a choice of mechanical, electronic, or control systems engineering. I chose mechanical which was taught in Cincinnati, Ohio. After graduation, I accepted a "permanent" assignment with the GE light military electronics group in Utica, New York. As part of the acceptance, I insisted on being admitted to the control systems C Course which was taught there.

When I left for graduate school, Gene finished his four-year USAF hitch and started in mechanical engineering at the University of Washington on the GI Bill. He stayed at Sherwood House. When he graduated, he went to work for GE in Pennsylvania. Lula graduated in journalism two years behind me and went to work for the Shelton weekly newspaper. In a few months, she met Jim Nichols, newly out of the navy in Bremerton, Washington. They married and moved to his hometown, Lodi, California. Their three children were David, Linda, and Carol. She got a job with the local welfare department and spent her career as a welfare caseworker.

Doris married Keith Simpson and eventually both of them and Leonard were working for the Simpson Logging Company. After Neil graduated from high school, he started working for Simpson's, bought a new Ford and crashed and died in 1956 trying to outrun the cops on a gravel road.

James Casteel and Eddie Cochran both became career navy enlistees. Buddy Knudsen joined his uncle's gypo (small) logging operation which he inherited when his uncle died. Both Buddy and Hewitt Slater married local girls. Hewitt got a job in Tacoma and spent his working career there. In 1960 Dad died in a car accident.

After three years in Utica, I got very tired of the upstate New York winter weather and joined a new GE radar engineering and marketing group co-located with a GE Advanced Studies group in Santa Barbara, California. In 1962, GE had a bad sales year and partially dismantled money losing operations including the Santa Barbara operation. I left GE and joined Aerospace Corporation, a non-profit advisory group formed by the USAF Space and Missiles commands. I subsequently learned that Westinghouse discontinued their Illinois Tech scholarship program a year after I graduated because too few graduates were joining Westinghouse and that GE had discontinued their advanced engineering program because too many graduates were leaving GE.

I met and married Patricia Green in Manhattan Beach, a suburb of Los Angeles in 1964, and spent my career and retirement in California. We had three daughters and a son (Deborah, Tamara, Elizabeth, and Roderick) who all graduated from college. In 1980, I left Aerospace and joined Lockheed in Sunnyvale, California.

I retired in 1999 and spent several more years as a consultant to Lockheed.

Gene married Hazel Lakim in 1954 and they had one daughter and two sons (Lisa, Edward, and Timothy).

Leonard married Ruth Mast in 1950 and they had a daughter and a son. (Susan and Mike) Leonard and Gene both retired at age 62.

Gene spent most of his career working for a GE heavy electrical switchgear unit in Houston, Texas. When he retired he left his two sons and daughter in Houston and moved back to Shelton. He bought Mom's 10 acres and built a house in the field near Cranberry Creek. At the time, Mom was 88 years old and living alone in our old house.

After her children were nearly grown, Lula divorced Jim Nichols and moved back to Shelton where she bought and lived in a house trailer for a while then let her younger daughter, Linda, move into it as she bought a house. In 1999 she rented her house to Linda's divorced husband and moved in with Mom to keep her company.

Doris and Keith had two sons and a daughter (Bradley, Brett, and Bridget) and raised them in a house in Shelton. Keith died of cancer in May 1979, and Doris worked at rural mail delivery, then for Simpson's for the next 20 years to support herself until she could collect Social Security and some retirement income.

The End